Entrepreneurial Mindset

A Pathway to Success for Immigrants

CORNELIUS DIPO AJAYI, MBA

Entrepreneurial Mindset

A Pathway to Success for Immigrants

PREVIOUS WORKS BY THE AUTHOR

1. My Book of Prayers

2. Jars of Clay

3. Our Book of Prayers for Couples

4. It's the Holidays Stupid! Time to Declutter Your Home

5. Parenting Your Children in a Technology Dominated World

Entrepreneurial Mindset

A Pathway to Success for Immigrants

Cornelius Dipo Ajayi, MBA

Entrepreneurial Mindset

A Pathway to Success for Immigrants

Copyright © 2021 Cornelius Dipo Ajayi, MBA

ISBN: **979-8-46465-170-8**

Book design: Pinon Creations
(+2347061150991)

All rights reserved. No portion of this book may be reproduced, stored in a retrieval system or transmitted, in any form or by any means electronic, mechanical, photocopy, recording or any other-without prior written permission of the publisher.

DEDICATION

This book is dedicated to all immigrants around the world who have seized the moment to start a business with their name on the door. Leaving your motherland to travel and live in another country is hard enough. To now start a business in your new country can be daunting. But many people have blazed the trail, unperturbed or intimidated by their limitations. Starting a new business can be tripping, sending your adrenalin up through the roof. You do not know what lies ahead but something instinctive keeps nudging you on until you look yourself in the mirror and say, "I have not done badly." Or, if you are a Christian, you say, "See what God has done!"

As the title says, "Entrepreneurial Mindset, A Pathway to Success for Immigrants" is also dedicated to those who are thinking about starting something of their own but are limited by a myriad of factors. The summation of those factors is FEAR. Fear of the unknown, fear of lack of money, fear of risking everything again after migrating from the motherland, fear of failure and all what not. This book is dedicated to you because somewhere on the pages is a prod, an inspiration and motivation to not give up but to take the leap of faith. In the words of Nike the shoe company's slogan, "Just Do It."

Finally, I'd like to dedicate this book to my wife and co-traveler in the business of immigrant entrepreneurship, Mariam Ajayi, a silent operator, motivator, and disciplined leader. Thank you again and again.

TABLE OF CONTENTS

DEDICATION vi
FOREWORD 9
PREFACE 12
ACKNOWLEDGMENTS 17
INTRODUCTION 19
Part 1 22
My Personal Entrepreneurial Story 23
CHAPTER 1 26
Deposing the Imposter 26
CHAPTER 2 30
Mind Filter; Shutting out the Naysayers 30
CHAPTER 3 35
Developing the Wealth Mindset 35
CHAPTER 4 40
Why you need to own a business 40
Part 2 51
CHAPTER 5 52
Find your problem 52
CHAPTER 6 58
Developing a Great Business Plan 58
CHAPTER 7 65
Finding your Funds 65
CHAPTER 8 73
Building your Team early 73

CHAPTER 9 79

The Power of Good Mentorship 79

PART 3 85

CHAPTER 10 86

The Power of Organization 86

CHAPTER 11 91

The Irreplaceable Power of Successful Public Relations 91

CHAPTER 12 96

Building generational wealth, the unrivaled glory of business owners 96

CHAPTER 13 102

Scaling your business and diversification 102

CHAPTER 14: 107

The importance of family 107

CHAPTER 15: 112

Last Words, TRLT! 112

ABOUT THE AUTHOR 118

FOREWORD

Every generation needs men and women who can stand out in the crowd to pursue a vision of starting something new. The risks can be daunting to those who are not fully motivated, but for those who have a mind of changing the course of the destiny of their lives and other people who depend on them, it is in the territory.

I am delighted to see Cornelius Dipo Ajayi, write a book on Entrepreneurial Mindset. I am particularly gratified that he focused on a familiar audience - the immigrant community. I believe that it would be a great resource for those who have yet to make up their minds about starting something that is entrepreneurial.

I know that many constraints confront a would-be business owner, not to mention the additional layer of challenges an immigrant would face. But it all boils down to a problem of mindset. There are mountains out there in the woods, but every person has a choice to say, I can climb, or I cannot climb the mountain. The reward for making the right choice can be satisfying and far reaching.

When Cornelius Dipo Ajayi and Mariam his wife decided to start their business in 2008 it was the height of the Great Economic Recession. Several years later, I am happy to see them succeeding where others have struggled or given up. That is what makes Entrepreneurial Mindset unique. It is not just about starting a business; it is also about riding the multiple waves that come in the journey. The mindset is a lifetime attitudinal behavior. Once you have a mindset of starting a business, you must extend it to the destination point.

Your desire must go beyond just owning a business venture, it must include where you want it to be in ten, fifteen, twenty years and more. In fact, you can think of your exit strategy from the start. Do you want to grow your business to the point where you can go public? Or you would like to build assets to the level of being able to sell the business for your retirement income? Maybe you are looking to pass on what you started to your heirs like Mr. Samuel Walton who founded the Walmart Company. Today, his descendants are continuing the legacy of what he started and bequeathed to them.

I believe that this book will point you in the direction of decision-making about your own entrepreneurial goals. As the author revealed in the last chapter of the book, business ownership is "A Road Less Traveled", yet it is a journey of immeasurable rewards if you have the right mindset.

I hope that you will join the community of those who have put aside the inconveniences and doubts; and like them, decide to create an enterprise with your name on it. This book will be a good resource in your plans.

Aderonke Mordi PhD, RN, MBA
President and CEO
International Quality Homecare / PCA
Omega Home Healthcare
International Properties, LLC
Rochester, Minnesota, USA

ENTREPRENEURS EMBODY THE PROMISE OF AMERICA: THE IDEA THAT IF YOU HAVE A GOOD IDEA AND SEE IT THROUGH, YOU CAN SUCCEED IN THIS COUNTRY, AND IN FULFILLING THE PROMISE, ENTREPRENEURS ALSO PLAY A CRITICAL ROLE IN EXPANDING OUR ECONOMY AND CREATING JOBS.

President Barack Obama

PREFACE

Several reports in the public domain reveal that whereas the immigrant population in America owns about 20% or more of businesses in the country, their population ratio is just 13%. That is to say that immigrants' ratio of business ownership is higher than by American born citizens. As a first-generation immigrant myself, I consider it incredibly useful to understand this fact, and in my own way, contribute to the body of knowledge about immigrant success in business ownership in God's own country. If anything, I want this book to be catalytic in getting more immigrants to become entrepreneurs in their new country.

Maybe you can identify with my antecedent in entrepreneurship; maybe you have been wondering if you can ever own a business with your name on the register. Seat back and let your mind settle down to assimilate the revelations in this book. Looking back, my foray into starting a business in America was more of a necessity than trying to prove a point. Granted that I had an MBA, and a stint in starting a company in Nigeria before migrating, none of those things motivated me more than my desire to own something of my own in the most entrepreneurial economy in the world. Talking about the Entrepreneurial Mindset, my number one drive and passion was to become an American employer of labor. I wanted to wear it as a badge of honor that I came to America and became an employer of labor. My passion increased in 2008, at the onset of the Great Recession. Job losses in the big corporations were skyrocketing and small businesses were being called upon to pick up the slack. Some organizations were, in fact, offering incentivized training to laid-off people to learn how to become self-employed or retrain for positions in the essential sectors that survived the recession. I was wondering what I could do to get people back to work in my own little way.

Avoiding naivety, I understood that the immigrant is exposed to a different set of challenges from the American born. This ranges from school attended, to accent of speech, access to capital, and what I call "the grand zero" experience which is unique to the foreign-born arriving in America. This experience humbles you beyond what you have prepared for in your new country. It is a cultural and economic shock that sometimes makes you feel unwelcome and unloved to the point of contemplating returning to your native country, especially if you have lived a modest life of success back where you came from. But then, you consider that you had spent all your savings in your country of origin to be able to come to America. Maybe you sold your car or house, or you gave up a plum job, with a few decent perks like paid club membership, a house and a chauffeur-driven car, a common practice in corporate life in third world countries, Nigeria in particular. Because of these limiting factors, the thought of going back has no place in reality, both economically and socially. For me, going back to Africa without appreciable success in the US would be a social and economic embarrassment.

If you came to the US with less privileges in your home country, a more predominant phenomenon, then you know that returning to your home country is not even an option. So, you decide to stick it out and wait for whatever lies ahead; after all, you are envied by your family and friends back where you came from for escaping the deteriorating state of things in your home country. In the meantime, you must feed your family, put a roof over them, and send your children to school. In many cases, this process involves doing myriad jobs and going back to school yourself to acquire an American diploma or professional licensure to improve your career chances.

Immigrants are known to do the menial jobs. From cleaning stadiums and shopping malls, to providing office assistance in corporations, it is often said that immigrants are here to do the minimum wage paying jobs. Pitiful as it may sound, this is the stage where many immigrants get the motivation to push themselves to the point of self-determination. Most of the cleaners, office assistants, nursing assistants and bank tellers, the entry level jobs in most cases, came to America with bachelor's degrees or even post graduate degrees. Some are PhD holders and medical doctors who are yet to secure their American practice license. Some never succeed in that endeavor and would have to decide what to do to make something out of their "grand zero experience".

Happily, America offers countless entrepreneurial opportunities for anyone who has the right mindset. It then becomes an issue of how hungry you are to become an employer, first of yourself, and of others. You also determine to pursue the American Dream in a more meaningful and resourceful way. Your passion and resilience, which have been useful in your "grand zero" years are now available again for your motivation and drive. A noticeable difference between a native born American and the immigrant in risk management is the level of "What do you have to lose?" In most cases, as mentioned earlier, you have given up everything you achieved in your home country and now, losing it again would not intimidate you. Also, in terms of inheritance, many Americans are in line for a chunk of money to be passed to them by their older parents and grandparents. Many have inherited or would inherit a house or two when their parents die. Several others are heavily invested in the stock market and have six to seven figure balances in their workplace 401ks.

As an immigrant, you don't have these luxuries or opportunities. Thus, poverty could be your motivating factor. Your children are growing up in your new country, passing from high school to college in just a few years. They amass high college loans which you cosign by force. The urge to escape the trojan of bi-weekly paycheck must be humbling enough that you are researching what else to do to earn extra income. You become one of the millions of people trying to hustle to earn extra income for their needs. Thank God, because of the explosion of the 21st century technology economy you don't have to think indefinitely. From becoming a Uber driver or Uber dinner delivery person, to doing freelance writing, to finding a spot in the thousands of opportunities in real estate selling, home health care, and insurance selling, you can absolutely find something to start with an affordable startup cost.

Second generation immigrants are faring even better. Although they struggle through college because of acculturation problems - what we call the sandwich culture - they are sharper in idea generation and know the entrepreneurial landscape more than their parents. Some of them are taught entrepreneurship and basic investing from high school. I was privileged to teach a students' business club in my children's high school, and I envied the smart ones among them who could gain advantage of future business ownership from what they were learning. I was convinced that this experience contributed to my son trying out a partnership venture in app development with some of his friends in college. He was also trying his hands on e-commerce retailing to augment his college money needs. Younger immigrants are well versed in business formation, building a team of startup founders, locating angel investors, and writing great business proposals. Definitely they are defter in using technology to create value, something that their first-generation immigrant parents know little about. As I write this book, I am deferring to my children on a regular basis to get their ideas and knowledge of several initiatives I am pursuing. They have always proven to be ahead of me and their Mother in entrepreneurial conversations. Let me also add that a large proportion of second-generation immigrants are exposed to higher levels of training and development which prepare them for entrepreneurship activities in a few years.

In a July 2019 report by the New American Economy Research Fund, titled, "Top American Companies and Their Immigrant Roots", it was found that 45 percent, or 223 companies, were founded by immigrants or their children. They included Amazon, Apple, Tesla, and Google parent company Alphabet, which are the leading companies in their categories.

In essence, the immigrant has many opportunities to pursue business ownership in the USA. What I think is lacking is the right mindset. There is the primary "I can't do it!" fear-factor, and the belief that there's not enough money to start something. Many people who have spoken to me about starting a business say they have no idea about how to go about it. I hope this book helps you to think better, deeper, and wider. In the final analysis, I pray that you get some motivation to go and start your own business so that you too can become an employer of labor in the most developed and prosperous nation on earth.

ACKNOWLEDGMENTS

There are many people who contributed to this book, some from the other side of the Atlantic Ocean. I got help from two of the leading online freelance organizations, Upwork and Fiverr, and multiple proofreaders including a friend in Johannesburg, South Africa. I am thankful to my children who organized a focused group session to pick the title and cover design. Participants in the focus group were drawn from Minnesota, Connecticut, Massachusetts, Texas, California, New York, Virginia, and Chicago, to mention a few. Many of the ideas generated in the session were incorporated into the final product.

The chosen cover design was produced by Nigeria-based artist, Jemimah Solomon-Sanu of Pinon Creations. I found our working together a great example of true intercontinental teamwork.

I would also like to appreciate our mentors in the business of immigrant entrepreneurship, Pastor Michael, and Dr. (Mrs.) Aderonke Mordi of Joseph Companies Group, owners of International Quality Homecare Corporation, Rochester Minnesota. Dr. Mordi generously provided the Foreword for the book. Thank you all.

ON MY OWN, I WILL JUST CREATE AND IF IT WORKS, IT WORKS, AND IF IT DOESN'T, I'LL CREATE SOMETHING ELSE. I DON'T HAVE ANY LIMITATIONS ON WHAT I THINK I COULD DO OR BE

Oprah Winfrey

INTRODUCTION

The first time I was invited to speak about my business and my unprecedented success as a black immigrant living in America, I didn't know what to say. After agonizing over my speech for weeks, and finally following the simple advice of my wife to just "do you", I went in and dominated a room in the Washington DC business summit for forty-five minutes. When I was done, one man walked up to me and gave me a mind-blowing experience that has contributed to me writing this book which you have in your hands right now.

This young, thirtyish black man walked up to me and asked me; "How did you do it?" Now, a lot of people might have just started spouting off things they had done to get to where they were, tasks and strategies, and stuff like that, but I knew that was not what he was asking me about. Because as much as I heard what he had said, I also heard what he had not said. And I could see the curiosity and hunger in his eyes as he sought an answer to a question, I believed he really wanted an answer to.

I did not see that hunger because I was overly observant, I saw it because I recognized that look from the mirror from several years ago just before I started. I recognized the immense hunger he felt at all the things I was doing that he hoped he could do and the resultant determination to finally take the plunge he was feeling as well as the fear of the unknown that had kept him in the rut he was in till now that had stopped him from stepping out all along. I saw the light dance in his eyes as those emotions flitted past, and I remember that mental rut like it was yesterday.

"By doing it." I finally answered him shrugging, because more than sounding sparse and mysterious, that was the whole truth really. I just got up and decided that all those variables did not really matter, and I was going to take the plunge.

Everyone who has had to start a business, or a new phase of their lives, or even made some changes to their present situation have all been faced with the same question; how to start. And when that is taken care of, we find that about forty-fifty percent of the work is already done.

My youngest daughter Deborah, who is already proving to be an entrepreneur in her own right at an incredibly young age, is a born storyteller. When asked about anything, she first gives you an interesting backstory before giving you a remarkably interesting play by play of the sequence of events. So, at dinner time when everyone talks about their days, we save hers for last because we are guaranteed a good laugh. Apparently, she has this friend, Sophia, who is very industrious and ingenious. The girl always has ideas about fun adventures they could take or activities they could start in school like a lemonade stand for the music club concert or a campaign for environmental hygiene where they could get to wash the parents and teachers' cars during the holidays. When she has these ideas, she shares them with her friends and that is all they would talk about for the next couple days till another idea pops in and they end up not doing anything about the previous ideas. This friend's ideas seem to always make an entrance into our dinner conversations whenever we ask her about her day. So, one day, I asked her why Sophia never got round to implementing any of her ideas.

"Because she always tells them to death I guess." That was my daughter's flippant reply as she went on to cut into her steak. In that moment, it struck me that was what a lot of people do to their brainchildren; they sometimes analyze it and talk about it till they snuff it right out. Many people never get round to doing the things they want to do or starting that business they build in their mind because they spend all the time talking logistics till they are blue in the face or till they talk themselves out of the ideas.

As I looked at that young man standing before me at the DC business summit, and the questions shining brightly through his eyes, I was curious about what excuses he had given himself for not starting out. Now, I am not saying analysis and proper business planning are not necessary for any business venture, they are in fact the heart and soul of any venture. But entrepreneurship is basically believing in your dreams enough that they come to life. The ensuing conversation I had with that young man birthed the chronicle of wisdom and experience that I would put down in this book.

I hope you stick around for the exciting ride that this experience would be.

Part 1
SOMEONE IS SITTING IN THE SHADE TODAY BECAUSE SOMEONE PLANTED A TREE LONG AGO

Warren Buffet
Biilionaire American Stock Investor and Majority Owner of Berkshire Hathaway

My Personal Entrepreneurial Story

A journey of a thousand miles begins with a single step.
Chinese Proverbs

In the summer of 2005, my wife and I with our three young children filed into the Don Bros coffee shop along University Avenue, St. Paul, Minnesota. We did not go there for midmorning coffee although we ordered a few lattes. We were there to inspire each of us to exercise our thinking faculty about our future careers in God's own country. At the end of that deliberate exercise, my wife and I were clear about our desire to own a family business in health care. She had just enrolled in school to become a nurse while I was growing my business in financial services.

On our arrival in the USA five years earlier, after fruitless attempts to get a job in advertising, my professional career back in Africa, I diligently engaged in online research on the best available opportunities for immigrants in America. I sadly gave up on my first career love and found that most sources recommended that immigrants in America should focus on either financial services or health care because those two offer them more potential pathways to succeed than any other lines. Under the former, an immigrant could be successful in banking, insurance or as a financial advisor. In the latter, you could be a nurse, doctor, or laboratory technician. This explains why many immigrants are predominantly in the insurance and health care fields. Two quick reasons can be adduced for this preponderance: the supply and demand ratio remain hugely at variance. The jobs are also relatively stable and secure, transferable and they pay decent wages. So, eight months into my American sojourn, after a myriad of "temp agency" positions, August 2001 to be precise, I joined the MetLife Insurance Company, then number 25 of Fortune 500 companies, and undoubtedly one of America's leading corporations. My career in financial services continued until 2009 during the worst economic recession which came like a hurricane at the tail end of President George W. Bush's second term. As a side hustle and safety net for my family income (and my emotional sanity, I must confess), I enrolled in the popular Certified Nursing Assistant (CNA) course at the Red Cross, Downtown Minneapolis. Here was I joining my wife in the nursing assistant world, the steppingstone for many immigrants to advance to more professional health care positions.

After passing the nursing assistant test, I secured a part time position at the Presbyterian Nursing Homes, Bloomington. This enabled me to continue my daytime job as a financial advisor. I was surprised that contrary to my preconceived negative attitude to the nursing assistant job, not only did I love it, but I also enjoyed the unthinkable high regards of my nurse supervisors, young Caucasian women who I was terrified could ruin my fledgling side hustle. I knew then that the sky was the limit to my potential. I also realized that I was seeing regular increments in my hourly rate of pay at Presbyterian which even more encouraged me to flip my negative thoughts and switch to the opportunity zone.

The opportunity came in July of 2008 through a phone call. One of my classmates at the CNA school of the Red Cross called me to ask for how she and her brother could open a healthcare company. She thought my disposition in the classroom and networking abilities should place me in a position to know how to start a business. Really? Indeed, she was right. My number one client in my financial services career had been mentioning in my ears a new business opportunity she was working on - selling a home care franchise, Homekeepers International out of Rochester Minnesota. I referred my classmate to my client. On the same day, I had an urge, something we call "Holy Spirit leading", to inquire about the franchise opportunity for my wife and me which I did. Soon after, we went to Rochester for a briefing session with other would-be investors.

The 2008-2009 Recession did not look like the best of times to start a new business. After all, businesses were shutting down all over the USA. By itself, the economic situation was a dissuader. But one line I took from the Homekeepers franchise briefing session was Dr. Aderonke Mordi's (the owner-CEO) repeated quote, "The Road Less Traveled!" The look on her face and her demeanor was quite revealing: Business ownership is not for the weak at heart and fearful. It is not a get rich quick adventure, nor a sprint. It is a painful journey that ultimately leads to a land that is potentially ladened with blessings and goodness. I remember asking for a timeline to breakeven or profit: five years, she said. We registered our business name, Dominion Resources, Inc with the Minnesota Secretary of State and secured our employer identification number "EIN", from the Internal Revenue Service, IRS.

We traveled to the geographical area of our new franchise, Glencoe MN, and found a small corner shop for our office. On January 2nd, 2009, we opened our doors as Dominion Resources, Inc, doing business as Homekeepers International, Glencoe Minnesota. As I am writing this, twelve years later, I can confirm that only a few can go through what we went through - months of juggling two jobs by each of us to pay our home mortgage and utilities, as well as run our fledgling office without additional income.

CHAPTER 1

Deposing the Imposter

Every morning you have two choices:
Continue to sleep with your dreams or wake up and chase them.
Anonymous, Pinterest

"The first person you have to get over with is yourself", those words have helped me through one too many indecisive positions every time I start out doing something I have never done before, and I get overwhelmed with the doubts and fears of starting.

One of the few lessons I picked up from psychology class in college is that human beings are a creature of habit and it takes a lot for us to adapt to any change, positive or negative. There seems to be plenty of scientific research about change and the human response to change and one of those results really jumps out at me: There are two kinds of change: the episodic change and the continuous change. Now, the human mind's natural reaction to any of these kinds of change or any disruption in its equilibrium at all is to try to get back to its normal state or 'ground zero'. This is exactly what happens with the episodic change, our mind scrambles immediately to get back to where it was before the disruption and get on with our lives. Now this is possible to achieve because the change is temporary like a loud noise or the crashing sound of sea waves.

But with continuous change, it is harder to do. This change involves continuous, increasingly serious, relentless, unpredictable change. This kind keeps us off our equilibrium for longer and our minds tend to view it as a sort of threat when in fact it is a good thing. In response to this threat, our minds often begin to regurgitate our fears, doubts and insecurities and bring them to the surface of our consciousness and if we let these fears settle in, could rob us of a chance to be extraordinary.

Most of these fears and doubts sometimes present themselves as the "Imposter Syndrome". This usually happens, every time you put yourself or your work out there and you take a big step out of your comfort zone, you first try to convince yourself that you do not deserve the recognition that could come with it and you are then faced with the terrifying fear that you are a fraud who isn't qualified to even do those things you claim you can do when there are better people more qualified for the job than you are. You start to feel like your achievements are by luck or chance and not from your obvious hard work. This horrible feeling most times creates a stagnancy in creativity and a sort of paralysis that aborts the dreams of the lesser motivated individual. It also creates a sort of toxic comfort in your stagnant position that we then call a 'comfort zone' so we never have to feel the discomfort of that change again.

Deposing the Imposter

When Shannon L Alder wrote that "Feelings are what you have, not who you are"; she could not have been righter. The good thing about this imposter syndrome is that it is just an expression of an emotion we are all familiar with, fear. And the thing with fear is that it only has as much power as we give it over us.

I developed this exercise for my associates and employees whenever I want them to take on a more daring task than they have ever been used to. I ask them one question; "What is the worst that could ever happen?" and I do not just stop there, I let them dispel with those fears by telling them how we would deal with each fear as they come. We find ways to be okay and even better after facing each of those fears till the possibility of them no more scares us. This exercise has in many ways not only destroyed the fears of my colleagues, but it has helped us devise great problem solving and crisis handling skills without even facing the real-life conditions of it.

At the beginning, the imposter syndrome may masquerade itself as a form of modesty and you may be lulled into believing it is a virtue to be lauded and not deposed. But the imposter syndrome does not do you any favors. It stifles your creativity and keeps you in a limbo worse than stagnancy. Here you know you should move on from where you are onto something better, but your fear of failing keeps you trapped in your previous position. Soon, basically you are experiencing what I call the creative unrest (which most times leads you to bigger innovations and greatness) but you do nothing about it until you are driven and motivated to free yourself from that state of mind.

The creative unrest was meant to make you uncomfortable in your former position so you could move on to the next level, but if the purpose of the creative unrest is defeated, then all you are left with is just discomfort without the birthing process that comes with it. From what I have come to realize by hearing different variations of the same story of "imposterism" (my vocabulary), is that if you are an entrepreneur, and you are always pushing yourself to places you have not been or places that intimidate you, then the imposter syndrome is a natural byproduct. If you have not felt like a fraud or grossly inadequate for the role you want to play, then you are doing it wrong, and you have probably stayed in the same place for a long time and gotten comfortable there.

You are probably asking me what to do about this paralyzing expression of fear, but the first thing I want you to know and understand is that that feeling of inadequacy, even though it has its negative effect, is not necessarily a bad thing. When you identify it for what it is; a creative unrest, then you are equipped with the ability to overcome it. This is your first step towards starting your own business and overcoming your greatest fear of failure.

Secondly, take some time for introspection and find out if those things you fear or feel inadequate about are true. In my life and career, building businesses and training other entrepreneurs, I have met a lot of people and four times out of ten, I have found out that if you feel like you are not qualified or know enough about a certain matter to be an authority in it, you are probably right. And because the first step in any form of growth is a moment of truth, you need to discover and acknowledge the truth about your capabilities and your knowledge. Advising you to take control of your situation and take a big plunge would never mean for you to not calm down and do all the required research, get all the required knowledge for your field. So be honest with yourself about what you do know and what you do not. And try as much as possible to gain that knowledge for yourself (see more on this in Chapter 13, the 8Ds of Entrepreneurial Mindset). If you need to employ the help of a professional to help you determine your next step, then by all means.

The first thing you need is passion and drive, the second is knowledge, the third is capital. No one said you need them all in perfect quantities, you just need enough to start, the rest will come later. And if you are worried about failure? It is just your first learning hub, because you could never do worse than your failures. One of my favorite business quotes by Michael Bloomberg is that "You must first be willing to fail, and you must have the courage to go for it anyway." I am a living witness to these imperfections and through a ruthless and deliberate effort, I won against my imposter syndrome and now I can tell you to do the same.

CHAPTER 2

Mind Filter; Shutting out the Naysayers

Stop being afraid of what could go wrong, and start being excited of what could go right.
Tony Robbins, Public Speaker, Bestseller Author

As a business owner who ventured out during the great recession of 2008/2009, I had to face not only the loud opinions of my own fears and doubts, I also had to face the negative energy from people around me.

I remember the first time I said out loud that if I ever had the opportunity to migrate to the US, I was going to be one of the most successful businessmen in God's own country and I would live the ultimate American dream. I was in a restaurant with one of my closest friends and it was the beginning of 1998, my wife was pregnant then with my daughter Deborah and I was half through my MBA program back in Nigeria. My friend gave me this look of astonishment, and pity along with a hesitant nod; then he said to me; "Hey Dipo, aren't you setting your sights too high? You do not even have an international passport or American visa. And you know what it is like for African Americans over there, let alone the fate of an immigrant. What with the weight of racism and all?"

Then he went on to spout a lot of reasons why those dreams I had should never see the light of day. And in all truth and earnestness though, he was right. Racism was still as thick as it had ever been, and the marginalization of immigrants was still very glaring. So, in truth, the possibility of getting out of my country into America and making a success out of it was slim. But as he was listing out all the things that could go wrong, I was envisioning everything that could work out and go right. So, while for a lesser man the possibility of failure would have put a halt in his step or even a pause to his plans, for me it made me work harder so that in the year 2000 with my wife and three children, and one thousand dollars in my name, I got into the United States and within twelve years, I built a business from scratch that has led me to writing this book.

From that one experience, I had to learn that when starting out, the only voice that mattered most of the time was mine. Not the voice of my fears or my doubts or even my bank account balance, not the voice of others who did not have a stake in my dreams and could not relate to my passion. Truly, my friend meant well. In his own way he was looking out for me, helping me weigh the pros and cons and helping me find the 'safer' option. My problem with the concept of safety would come in a totally different story, but in this one incident a lesson I had taken for granted for awfully long came to the fore: your dreams are as valid as you make them. The world around you will only take you and your dreams as seriously as you take yourself.

I had to get used to the fact that there would be a line of people round the block who had a lot of things to say about my business and my plans and all their words would be negative. I had to learn the hard way to not let their words affect me so much, even when those words would come from people I loved and cared about, people like my friend. I remember my friend coming to my apartment on a Saturday afternoon and while we were kicking back after lunch, I had laid out my plans for him.

"You really are serious about this?" he asked, the incredulous look in his eyes hard to miss. I gave him a flippant yes and he said something that I probably would never forget for the rest of my life; he voiced one of my biggest fears. "Dip Dip, how would you guys even get the capital? Do you plan on raising these kids on minimum wage till your business picks up? What if you fail? You're not just thinking about yourself or even your wife anymore, there are three kids in the equation to think about and put into consideration."

I need you to understand how I felt when he said those words to me; my friend and I have always been very frank to each other. He was my sounding board when it came to my ideas and whenever I needed someone to help me put things into perspective, he was the best person for the job. I could count on him to put sentiments aside and give me great advice. So, suffice it to say that I valued his opinions a lot and having him point out the exact same holes I had noticed in my own time and acknowledged to myself, it almost took the wind out of my sails.

In the end though, I had to choose what was more important to me, which risk I could live with. I was running the risk of abandoning my plans and regretting it later or taking my big plunge and risking failure in the long run. Jeff Bezos, the famous founder, and CEO of Amazon said, "I knew that if I failed, I wouldn't regret that, but I knew the one thing I might regret is not trying!" Well, we all know the choice I had made that led to this book you have in your hands now. It was not an easy decision, and quitting was looking very attractive as time went by, but it took a lot of soul searching and clarity of purpose and direction to stay the course and go on with my plans.

It hits differently when your naysayers are your family or respected friends and advisers and learning to shut them out and do your thing takes a lot of courage. The truth is that these people who would ruthlessly come after your business ideas and your plans would care deeply about you and the harder they care, the harder they would fight to keep you safe and out of risk. This does not however call for you to alienate them and label them bad, the truth is that naturally, human beings are averse to risk and we tend to fight to stay in situations that are comfortable. But as an entrepreneur, you have become a risk taker by default and as you make provision for their failings, you should never let them talk you out of a lifetime opportunity.

As a matter of fact, even other entrepreneurs who are also self-starters would try to discourage you when you want to start your own business. They are more difficult to handle because they know firsthand the struggles you are about to face, and they will try to dissuade you from leaving that nine-to-five job that gave you a false sense of security. They would try to tell you how difficult it is to pursue your dreams and because they know the risks, they would tell you not to venture into that small business in an uncharted territory.

The first thing I learned in finding my own way and defining my own journey was defining for myself what success meant to me. This is because for a lot of people - some of your naysayers inclusive - a safe job with stability and enough money for a mortgage and a minivan sounds like the definition of success and they would look at you like you have gone crazy for wanting to give that up. Success means a lot of different things for different people; it could mean getting to the top of the corporate ladder. It could mean the security your job gives you. It could mean a house in the Bahamas and a fancy yacht. It could also mean having more time to spend with your family, or not having to work for someone else in your life ever again.

Every entrepreneur I have met has expressed one wish and I think that is the one thing all entrepreneurs have in common; living the life they always wanted on their own terms, not having to answer to anyone else. While this may not exactly be their definition of success, it is the starting point to a path that would lead them there.

Secondly, I had to determine when to stop listening to people around me and determine who to listen to. No small business owner or self-starter thrived without the help of experts and consultants in their field. However, the beauty of doing it yourself is having the choice of taking all the 'advice' you get with a pinch of salt. You should be teachable and ready to learn from even the unlikeliest of people. But you must understand and draw the line between being objective, keeping an open mind and being gullible. You would be doing yourself and your business a huge amount of good if you can sit down and learn, but you should draw the line between genuine professional business opinions and the projection of fear and doubt from your naysayers. Learn to discern who to pay attention to and who to ignore. You would not have to alienate them, after all they mean well. Make provisions to forgive them for doubting your capabilities and intelligence and thank them for their concern, but you should never let anyone talk you out of greatness.

CHAPTER 3

Developing the Wealth Mindset

Wealth building is not a sprint, it is a marathon. The Entrepreneur who is looking for a get-rich quick strategy has the wrong mindset and may end up terribly disappointed.
By the Author

One of the biggest reasons for a lot of people to become entrepreneurs is the hunger to become financially independent along with the need to solve a problem. The entrepreneur's priorities determine which one of these needs come first. But to be able to develop true wealth and financial liberation, developing a wealth and abundance mindset is very crucial.

A lot of people think they know what a wealth mindset is or have a vague idea of what it means but when you ask ten people to define a wealth mindset to you on the spot, you would probably get ten different answers. And that is because people believe strongly that a wealth mindset has something to do with their definitions of wealth and abundance. But what makes a wealth mindset so important is that no matter how much money means to you, it would still mean the same thing.

The first misconception about having wealth is that only people with millions in their bank accounts are rich. A wealth mindset is basically a set of beliefs, habits and behaviours that separate the truly wealthy from the rest. A wealth mindset will guide you to maximize your resources and make the most of the money you have. It is basically having the consciousness and thinking from a place of abundance. It basically means spending less, making wise investments, and finding ways to improve and grow your wealth with minimal risks.

One of the questions I get asked very often when talking about the wealth mindset is the difference between a wealth mindset and just gaining financial intelligence. Well, they are vastly different concepts. Financial intelligence is the ability to make good decisions about your money and your investments and knowing what to invest in. It is basically gathering information about the financial state and condition of corporate and financial entities to understand their nature and abilities to predict their intentions and make informed decisions.

A wealth mindset is very crucial to any small business owner because it would be what sets his or her business apart and determines where the business would be in the years to come. But then, this mindset does not come easy, it means spending less, making wise investments, and practicing delayed gratification.

I once sat in on a seminar one evening a few years back when issues about building wealth in small businesses were raised and one man stood and asked the speaker the relationship between having a wealth mindset and excelling as a small business owner. The speaker smiled and said, "The best way I know to describe this to you is with this analogy. Two men started their respective small businesses and with the hope of financial independence, they poured themselves into their work. A couple years into their ventures, the businesses started doing well and turning in a lot of revenue. The first man went ahead and started to buy a lot of fancy things; a house in the wealthiest part of town, a Porsche, and an expensive vacation. The other man however, found ways to put his revenues back into the business and invest in other side businesses. It should not surprise anyone that ten years down the line the first businessman had to declare bankruptcy while the other business owner had grown into a franchise and had several other startups on the side. I don't need to tell you who had the wealth mindset."

Now to understand more deeply what the man meant about abundance mindset, let us look at the way these two men thought about and analyzed their previous situations. The first man probably grew up in lack and he had a lot of things he felt like he needed but could not afford and he felt the first sign of success in his business was being able to afford those things. He felt there was no way he could afford those things otherwise. The other man however, though he also grew up with lack, decided to analyze his situation and invest his money wisely, practicing delayed gratification. I do not have anything against buying things you feel you need, but the mindset that there would not be more from where it came from is the problem.

Thinking about wealth makes all the difference in your financial decisions when starting a business. It would determine what kinds of investments you would make, who you partner with and how reliable you are with your resources and the resources of the people who have taken the chance on your business.

In contrast though, and for the sake of more clarity, I would like to explain what a poverty mindset means and represents. The first red flag that indicates that someone could have a poverty mindset is they think earning money is wrong or they believe in fast and quick money. They believe you can make money without working hard or with minimal effort. They also believe that they cannot climb out of their rut of financial misery and try to organically build their own wealth by themselves. They are basically quitters in plain clothes. This mindset will most likely guarantee that wealth is very far from any such one's life and abode.

The good news is that an abundance mindset, like a lot of behavioral and character adjustments, can be learned. It only requires hard work, a lot of studying and strategizing. Below are a few habits of truly wealthy people so we could study and emulate:

- **Patience:** Any process of growth is organic and takes time and we are encouraged to enjoy the process and learn from it. I do not know anyway how people think that growing wealth is any different. A lot of get rich quick schemes and ponzi schemes have made their fortunes from gullible lazy people who believe that growing wealth could be spontaneous instead of slowly. No big business name you hear today grew overnight, so sit down and make your plans painstakingly then trust the process to make you the wealth you desire.

- **Learn to invest:** Another hard thing a lot of small business owners have not learned to do is investing the returns from their business. A mentor of mine called investing the business of delayed gratification. A popular saying goes that you are not truly rich if you cannot have your businesses make money for you in your sleep. This does not necessarily mean you should sacrifice your sleep and health to build your wealth. The best way to have your business bringing in returns even in your sleep is by sending your revenue on a money errand. No wonder, Mr. Warren Buffet, America's premier stock market investor says that "If you don't find a way to make money while you sleep, you will work until you die!" When you invest, your money is compounding and starts to multiply itself. This process also needs patience because the longer you let that money sit in your account, the more returns you will make from it. Investing is a noticeably big strategy for the truly wealthy, they don't feel the need to spend it as soon as it is made. As a matter of fact, our business in home health care initially purchased a franchise with money my wife and I saved in our 401ks, an investment retirement plan you make for yourself with your employer where they offer the plan. So, you could only imagine what would have happened had we not decided to invest in our retirement plans. We would not have been able to seize on the opportunity when the offer came to us in 2008.

- **Invest in yourself:** The next thing you need to know is that making and sustaining wealth demands a lot of learning and information. And because there is new information in the market every day, it is even more crucial that as a thriving business owner, you must study twice as hard to develop and improve yourself. This would require you to minimize or stop altogether time-wasting habits like watching television, at least until you are successful. Maximize the time you spend on your communication gadgets. Instead of spending your time scrolling through cute baby or doggy pictures on YouTube, you could use that time to watch an educational video. More than money, the world is ruled by information and a lot of people are willing to pay a good amount of money for the knowledge you have. So, the years after you have established yourself in your business, it is not the time to rest on your laurels, it is actually the time for you to improve yourself.

Now, this may sound like a lot of work, but no great outcome ever comes from anything less than a great effort.

CHAPTER 4

Why you need to own a business

The biggest risk is not taking any risk. In a world that's changing really quickly, the only strategy that's guaranteed to fail is not taking risks.

Mark Zuckerber, Facebook founder/CEO

Benefits for you and all.

1. **The potential for higher income:**

    There is a belief that if everything goes well in a business enterprise, the owners would be rewarded with a decent profit for their investment and labor. It is a law of numbers that if one man or woman is in a paid employment, he or she and the co-workers will get paid because as the scripture says, "A worker is deserving of his wage." The multiplier effect of several workers means that as each worker helps the owners to generate a business income out of which he is paid, the small savings from each worker's effort become the business owners' pot of income. How does this happen? The owners apply reasonable economic principles of cost and benefits that allow them to retain some of the business income generated by the workers. Out of the remaining collective income, they pay taxes to the relevant authorities, as taxes on the wages paid to the workers, and as a reasonable share of the profits to the government. Do not be surprised to hear that your business will be sharing profit with the Treasury Department! It is how America keeps the engine of government running north, south, east, and west. The ability of the business owners to pay taxes to the government confers on them the legitimacy to keep the leftovers as net profit. Year over year, as the enterprise continues to grow and expand, the owners also grow and can accumulate assets, some in retained earnings, some in buildings, vehicles and other current assets of bank balances and stock investments. They also accumulate liabilities in bank loans and working capital, fixed assets that have not been fully paid for, such as mortgage loans, car notes and investors' funds. The world's billionaires are mostly business owners and entrepreneurs whose stock ownership in their businesses has grown over the years. Think of Mark Zuckerberg of Facebook who, within 10 years, skyrocketed to the top 10 of the richest people in the world. Think of Elon Musk of Tesla, Bill Gates of Microsoft, Warren Buffet of Berkshire Hathaway and Geico. Not to forget the number one richest family in America, the Waltons, descendants of Sam Walton the founder of Walmart which has at least three billionaires in the top 100 Richest Americans. Alice Walton, one the trio, is America's richest woman. Think also of the richest, single individual of many years running, Jeffrey Bezos of the online retail juggernaut, Amazon. His former wife, MacKenzie Scott is now the second richest woman in the US, because of the growth of the money she received from their divorce settlement. Now, think about this, after a divorce, both former spouses are billionaires!

The truth is that each of these prosperous men and women achieved their success through their entrepreneurial acumen. They could have been successful in paid employment in government or as top managers in their corporations, but they will not have had the financial power that they now command. All things considered; a business owner would be more financially successful than a worker in a paid job. There is a caveat. As they say, "Rome was not built in a day". Becoming financially successful in business is not a 200-yard sprint, it is a marathon! The Entrepreneurial Mindset is not a magical wand or get-rich-quick fallacy. It is not a casino or horse race bet. It is a thinking process that inspires the owners to work hard, make sacrifices and apply unique values and judgment to their decision-making activities. Over time, from humble beginnings, they would begin to realize their dreams. Maybe this is how the "American Dream" euphemism emerged. In any case, nothing compares to achieving the American Dream, or European Dream, or Asian Dream, or African Dream, than owning your own business.

2. **An Opportunity to Lift Your Family out of Poverty.**

Not many people were born into wealth, maybe only a fraction of the top 1% of the rich. Everyone else strived to become successful. Millions of families are getting by, from humble or meager incomes. Just as America has the billionaire class, it also has the middle class. Then there is another class called "below poverty line", a categorization that is in each population census. You will be surprised how many families are in this terrible category. Every country would have this class. In fact, third world countries have swaths of their populations in the "below poverty line" category. One of the characteristics of this group is that they are considered dependent on government stipends. During the height of the COVID-19 global pandemic in the summer of 2020, many countries released large amounts of money they called "palliatives." We saw terrible pictures of Nigerians in large spaces like football stadiums being thrown quarter bags of rice and beans, and boxes of sugar. One of the determinations an immigrant man or woman in America should make is that they would escape the poverty line and move up. It is a humbling experience to be at the mercy of counties, state, and federal agencies for your sustenance. There is also the urgency to extend the rescue mission of poverty alleviation to your relatives back in your home country. It should be your prayer that when your help is needed, you will not be in hiding. Business ownership may be your sure way to achieve this goal. Do not get me wrong, paid employment is not bad; the only problem is that you will have to wait for the next paycheck to know what to do. God knows, you may be living from paycheck to paycheck, meaning, you are unable to help anyone here or there. You can get out of the limitations of a paid job by starting something of your own, when the time is right, and you have the wherewithal to launch.

3. **Freedom to do what you love and be in charge of your destiny.**

When I was a junior Financial Advisor, I used to look in amazement, the senior Financial Planners telling us at group training events how we could afford to work four days a week or less; how we could play golf on Friday morning and be at the clubhouse for lunch. Because they had put a lot of work into their practice, and much more so because they had junior advisors like me working under them with administrative assistants, they could afford to do it. A senior planner would usually have a large section of the office floor to themselves, a secretary in charge of setting up appointments, an administrative assistant in charge of preparing documents for presentation to clients, and a few advisors doing research and a myriad of other tasks. All those tasks distributed among 6-7 people we, the juniors, had to do on our own. We worked 6.5 days a week and still needed more hours to accomplish much.

Permit me to say this: owning your own business does not guarantee success to become free from work. But at least, you oversee your own destiny. When we started Dominion Cares in 2009, for the first year and half, we combined working in the office, 50 miles away from home, with part time positions near home in the evenings and weekends. By the middle of 2010, we decided that my wife should go back to a full-time position in her nursing job to earn more money for our bill payment while I focused 100% on the running of Dominion. We brought her back full time to Dominion another 2 years later as we picked up more growth. Soon, we were able to take vacations together, like a week for family retreat in Florida, two weeks medical mission to Nigeria, and a few more weekend get-away. We began to feel a sense of freedom, not from working, but from work. The cool thing was that all my travels and vacations were work-included. I remember one time traveling with my 27" screen computer to enable me to do payroll with the computer. Many times, I did not set up "Away from the office" notification in my Outlook email. Someone might say, "That is not a holiday!" You are right; but it is always the best time of my life. I relax, I treat myself to good food, I call my office to discuss progress, and most of all, I write books.

I stopped reporting to a boss or supervisor and no longer feared being "written up" or facing disciplinary action for a lapse I did not commit. Do not get me wrong. These things are not evil, but they just do not give you the kind of liberty you have in running your own boat. You can afford to keep a flexible schedule. You can decide to work from anywhere if you are able to continue reaching the members of your team and customers. This has become more realistic in the aftermath of COVID-19 pandemic and work-from-home realities in almost all sectors.

I must admit that freedom to do what you like comes with a responsibility. First, you do not begin to see that freedom until your business starts to make profit! You cannot claim to be free if you have debts to your banks, credit card companies, and worst of all, the IRS! Between 2012- 2015, I enjoyed a melodramatic kind of freedom. We owed the IRS close to $50,000 in unpaid FICA - withholding taxes and Social Security, Medicare, and Federal Unemployment taxes. By the time we were done paying, we must have paid over $100k, thus robbing us of scarce working capital. When you carry debts in your business, it follows you to restaurants, beaches, and orchestra performances. Well, it follows you to church where you pray to God to set you free! Freedom also demands that you continue to show interest in your operations. You cannot abandon your role. I was on a medical mission trip to a small town in Nigeria one time when my phone rang. It was a call for a referral for a new client with many questions that my office wanted me to answer. I took the call at lunch time by walking away from the crowd to the open field nearby.

I will always remember me walking up and down answering those questions and watching for small snakes under the grass. But when it was all over, I felt a sense of Deja vu! I was still part of the team in my American office, I did not let down my staff who needed me to answer questions only meant for me. That is the kind of freedom I am talking about. Be where you are but do what you need to do, including keeping your responsibility to your business unhindered. This is how the thought of "From Your 8am - 5pm Cubicle to CEO Suite" came up as the alternative title for this book.

4. **Become an employer and put people to work.**

According to the Small Business Administration's 2019 report, America had 30.7 million small businesses and they employed 47.3 percent of the private workforce.

How about you trying to be one of those employers, and not one of those employees? Hello. At the point I migrated to the US in September 2000, my company in Nigeria had a workforce of 25 people after three years of starting. So, in America, although I started in entry level positions, I kept my ID card with my title of CEO in my closet at home where I saw it often and reminded myself that I would pick up that title again, sooner or later. One of the yardsticks for success in small business is how many people you can pull from the job market and help them to earn a living for themselves and their families. When we started Dominion, I saw a glimpse of that dream coming to fruition. Then I would tell my wife that nobody was earning $20k in salaries, we needed to work harder to hire more qualified people. Between 2012 and 2015, we were stuck at just about $25,000 in salaries and wages every two weeks. We stopped talking about it and with prayer, and more hard work, our payroll tab increased to $30k, then $40k, then $50k, every two weeks! Our payroll before the outbreak of the Coronavirus comprised 103 employees. That number dipped to 90 because of the COVID-19 restrictions and we are climbing back. In any case our payroll dollar amount continues to grow because now we have higher earning staff, including several in full time positions. That is a dream come true for me.

When you can add one person to your staff at the beginning, you will feel an air of accomplishment. We started with a 3-day a week office assistant, then 5 days a week, then two office assistants, then this and then that. Unless you have investors, who set you up for a big operation from the start, you will have to grow at your own pace. Do not envy nobody. I did not feel comfortable earning a salary until 5 years into our business. But, to the glory of God, we never, never missed paying our employees every two weeks. Paying your employees their wages is your priority as an employer. If you cannot pay your people, and you want to be a business owner, then opt for the "Solepreneurship" and handle all your tasks yourself. But even handymen need help running their offices, taking orders and processing bills. If you stay focused and do not expect early profits but hope for a rainy day, you will make it. Like our mentor answered me when I asked how long it would take to break-even in our business, I will also say to you, 5 years! If you do not see profit in 5 years, and you believe in your vision, call in a consultant to reevaluate your business model and processes. He/she will tell you what is needing tweaking and soon you will begin to see improvement.

Some organizations grow by the number of employees, some by the revenue they generate, yet some others, by the profit they record at the end of the year. I use all the yardsticks to measure our success and growth. But the greatest one that gives me the greatest optimism is the number of our staff. I will say my goal in business ownership is to help put Americans to work, year in, year out. I will keep pursuing this dream to the last day.

5. **Increase your capacity for generosity**

   I remember when we went to the Homekeepers Franchise information session in 2008 in Rochester Minnesota. Pastor Michael Mordi, the co-owner of the franchise (with his wife, Dr. Aderonke Mordi, of course) said to us, "Owning your own business will allow you to give more to your church and other Christian groups." Nothing can be farther from the truth. In America, your tithes, and offerings to your church and nonprofit organizations with a 501(c) tax exempt status are considered tax deductible. You can claim as much as you donate in the following year's taxes, but you must show your tax preparer, proofs of receipts from your receiving organizations. As a business owner, you want to maximize the tax-deductible opportunity as much as you can. This is where business ownership always trump being a salaried worker. We are all endowed with the spirit of generosity, but business owners have more realistic ways to give more than anyone else in their ranks. It becomes impudent on them, in the word of scriptures, each of you should give what you have decided in your heart to give, not reluctantly or under compulsion, for God loves a cheerful giver. *8And God is able to bless you abundantly, so that in all things at all times, having all that you need, you will abound in every good work. (2 Corinthians 9:7-8). (2 Corinthians 9:6-11, NIV)* If the Holy Scriptures say if you give generously, you will be made rich, you better believe it and strive to give generously for the sake of your business. In other words, business ownership should empower you to be more generous in your philanthropic giving. Start small and as your business grows, increase your giving.

Lastly, if you can pay the IRS hundreds of thousands of dollars in taxes on your profits, why can't you give some money to your church and Christian association which helps to reduce your tax liability?

6. **Help those who are close to you and become a global philanthropist.**

One of the blessings of business ownership is the opportunity to support charity organizations like churches, ministries, schools, and organizations engaged in missionary work abroad, and enjoy the benefits of tax deduction. Although you cannot claim money you give to your parents and family members as gifts or upkeep money, your increased income potential may enable you to be more generous. As your business grows and becomes more successful, you are in a good position to have more disposable income. You can take some of your annual profits to give to people who are close to you as a form of help like school fees, paying down a loan or deposit for a car or real estate purchase. These will make you and your beneficiaries feel a sense of community and interdependence. To maximize the tax-deductible benefits of money that you give to family members and non-profit organizations, you will need to seek the advice of your tax accountant or a licensed financial advisor who is familiar with the subject of stewardship and generosity. Just do not give out money and expect to be able to deduct it all. There are rules that guide charitable donations but with good advice, you can absolutely derive tax advantages.

7. **Put your leadership skills to profitable use.**

A business owner invariably is a leader. Every day as you make decisions about your operations, you will realize that you need to be wiser and introspective. You can afford to stumble for a while but not for too long. Entrepreneurial skills must include leadership qualities of good judgment, ability to listen to varying views, including those who do not agree with yours, knowledge of money management and a variety of skills in HR, marketing, and production. You will probably be a jack of all trades in the beginning. Knowing how to navigate through the various aspects of your business will be needed at this stage. As you plow along, you will notice that you are building leadership acumen which will help you first, in leading your fledgling employees as well as prepare you for the future when you are going to be looked upon to make bigger decisions. At this level, you will be expected to become more astute and shrewder. Entrepreneurship is a school. You launch into it and continue to grow as your business grows. You do not have to grow alone. You can find resources to help you like training and mentoring support.

Maybe you have other reasons for wanting to explore entrepreneurship. Maybe your parents owned a Mom and Pop or brick and mortar business in your home country and you think you would like to extend the DNA and even do better in America or wherever you are in the diaspora. Whatever it is, get motivated. Do not procrastinate. Take the leap of faith and launch. As they say, the journey of a million steps starts with the first step out of the door. Go for it.

Part 2

THE ENTREPRENEUR ALWAYS SEARCHES FOR CHANGE, RESPONDS TO IT, AND EXPLOITS IT AS AN OPPORTUNITY.

Peter Drucker, Management Consultant, Educator and Author

CHAPTER 5

Find your problem

"Great leaders are almost always great simplifiers, who can cut through argument, debate and doubt to offer a solution everybody can understand."

Colins Powell, Former United States Secretary of State

A couple of years into our business, a friend approached me and asked, "how do you know how much you're worth and how much you should charge your clients that will be fair?" I understood that question wasn't as much for me as it was for my friend's benefit. This question is one of the more frequently asked questions I have received, especially from entrepreneurs who sell services instead of tangible products. This question is often fueled by how they feel about their work and their confidence in creating value.

Money, payment, or financial compensation for your work is not just given to you because of your personality; it is provided as a result of the value you have given them. So, in essence, value births wealth or income, and what determines the value you're providing is the problem you are solving. You cannot create wealth (lasting wealth) without solving problems, but you give value without finding a problem to solve.

Robert Kiyosaki in one of his many bestseller books about entrepreneurship and business, said, "in every problem lies an opportunity." And he couldn't have been more right. Every big brand ever talked about in the business world came to the limelight by solving pressing societal problems.

When Jeff Bezos started Amazon, he only had a problem he was passionate about solving and a garage in his parent's house. He stumbled upon a startling statistic when he was in New York City working for a qualitative hedge fund that the usage of the World Wide Web was growing at two thousand, three hundred percent by the year. Then he went about looking for a business plan that would solve a problem that came with this opportunity. One thing people are not often told is that even though in every problem lies an opportunity and a solution, every solution births an even bigger problem that would need a more prominent solution. Thus, wealth is secured for every visionary individual who knows how to leverage problems instead of being afraid of them.

However, Bezos decided to make life easier for the consumers of the internet and help bring them the products they would otherwise have to go out of their way searching for to their doorstep. Now, before his idea, the notion of commercializing the internet was inconceivable to people around the world. However, Jeff Bezos decided he wanted to get people an 'everything store' according to the first name he gave his business Cadabra after the magic word Abracadabra. Still, he had to change it because a colleague mistakenly called his business 'cadaver,' so the name had to go. The point, though is, he found a compelling problem he wanted to solve to make the lives of people more comfortable.

Before Larry Page and Sergey Brin founded Google from their dorm room in Stanford University, California, in 1998, there were other search engines already in use by the public, namely, Yahoo, Lycos, AltaVista, etc. But when these two grad students started, they quickly gained the general public's attention and gained the attention of the academic community and the Silicon Valley investors. They did all this by creating a search engine that used links to determine the importance of individual pages on the World Wide Web, an engine they initially called Backrub.

They soon became one of the top 5 companies in America with the highest-grossing net profit. And all this because they found a way to make the website search more straightforward and organized so you are not faced with an overload of information at the click of a button, but you deal with focused and organized searches and answers.

I know many people's default reaction to this would be to ask how to know which significant problem they could find and how to tell if it will be as useful to others as you make it to be. For the rest of this chapter, I will try to show you how to know the important questions to ask when you have found a problem and how to know your problems when you see them.

Caring About People Genuinely

Suppose you are primarily in the service industry; in that case, you must be familiar with the phrase 'the customer is always right.' Although this phrase only vaguely connects to the point being made here, this is a reminder that the most important person in every entrepreneurship business is the people. Your clients and customers are the most important people, and your business revolves around them. Whatever problem you set out to solve, it must have the people at its center. You know you have a worthy problem when the society's structure gives you concern or makes you indignant about the state of the people around you. This then keeps your mind's wheels turning till you find a solution, something that would help make life easier for them. So, the first thing you need is a problem that keeps you awake and makes you want to help the people around you.

And by caring about people, I mean you must be genuine about it. There are things about life you just cannot fake, and real emotions are one of them. Get involved in the lives of the people around you, be curious about them. At the inception of smartphones, Samsung and Apple companies were the pioneers of the market. However, there was still one big problem, the Japanese company that owns the Tecno brand of mobile phones discovered that problem from clients' reviews that many people loved the phones made by Samsung and Apple companies. However, they could not afford it because of its high prices, and they could not carry more than one smartphone to accommodate their other sim cards. So, they came up with a solution; a smartphone that had multiple sim card slots and all the features of a smartphone at a very affordable rate. This was how they infiltrated the African market and started slowly dominating it. If they had not been interested in knowing what people were saying about the products, their name and brand might still not be mainstream as it is now.

Finding the Root Cause of Your Problem

For this part, I would like to borrow a phrase from the Holy Bible where it says and I quote, "If anyone wants to set out to build a house, they have to sit down and count the costs, and only when they are done should they start building." This I find to be true for every venture anyone is embarking on. No one truly sets out to build a house without first sitting down to decide the motive for building it in the first place, then the purpose of the building down to the individual rooms. They will then invite professionals, surveyors, lawyers, building contractors, etc., to find out what it would take and how much it would cost, and the project goes on.

This, in turn, applies to your problems in a business. In an earlier chapter, I mentioned that you need passion and a vision you believe in to be able to fire up yourself and your team. Your passion is fueled by how strongly you feel about the problem you discovered. But what gives you a compelling vision is the research you put into your problem to find out the root cause of the problem. Asides from observing the problem to know its patterns and what makes it so problematic, you have to decide the root cause of the problem.

You cannot provide a solution on a weak foundation. You must research your problem, find out if anyone has ever tried to solve it before. If yes, why did they fail? If no, then why has no one seen it or attempted to solve it? Here the issue of genuinely caring about people comes up again. You cannot find the root cause of your problem with a superficial study. You must go deep and research extensively, talk to the people who have the problem or who you feel it affects deeply. I call this exercise getting your hands on the pulse. Find out if there is even a need for a solution for this problem, or you might just go into business providing a less desirable option for a problem that does not even exist or already has a solution.

Even if the problem already has a solution, you can go on to research the people already in that market. And you do not just do that by imitating them; you study their solution to the problem, find out what they are doing wrong and try to fix it. Then and only then will you be considered a worthy competitor in the market. Defining the problem properly gives you an edge in the market so that you are not just another start-up around the block.

Coca-Cola is arguably the leading beverage brand in the food and drinks industry because it has managed to stay relevant in the market and ahead of the curve. With a lot of other brands trying to imitate the Coke formula, it would have been easy for the company to fade into obscurity or just become another name on the block. However, their formula still stays unique and well sought after.

Leveraging the Trend

The next big thing you must know about finding a problem is trends. We have already established that to find your problem's root cause, you must care about the people sincerely and listen to them. And the best way your potential clients can speak to you is through trends. Human beings are very social beings, and one of the things that makes this true is the nature of their emotions. We are usually moved by what is going on and what everyone else is talking about. Therefore, it is crucial to have your hands on the pulse all the time. It is essential as a start-up to keep up with the latest trends in technology, communication, marketing, customer service, and any other areas that would affect your business.

Jeff Bezos started Amazon.com to deal with his regret for not leveraging the internet when it came out when he saw the overwhelming information going about internet usage. So, he went on to find a way to leverage the opportunities created by the internet. People still loved to read books, and with the advent of getting information on the web, the most obvious solution was to find a way to get them the books they wanted to their doorstep without anyone leaving their houses to go get them. Then he got on the second most sought-after product, music. People loved to be entertained by a good song, and music CDs were a rave then, so he started selling them too, and soon after, everything could practically be sold on Amazon.

When people started spending most of their time on social media to amass more entertainment, business owners decided to get on those social media platforms, too, selling their products with a little bit of entertainment and engagement thrown in. I could go on and on, but I think I have made my point. You could very easily find a problem you are passionate about from seeing things through the eyes of the people whose business you want. Nothing shows you are genuinely interested in them other than understanding what makes them tick. Business, after all, is the science of knowing people and delivering a solution to their needs.

CHAPTER 6

Developing a Great Business Plan

Without a plan, even the most brilliant business can get lost. You need to have goals, create milestones and have a strategy in place to set yourself up for success.
Yogi Berra, Former American professional baseball catcher, Manager and Coach

A cliché goes that "Most people don't plan to fail, only that most people fail to plan!" Incredible isn't it? When one fails to plan, it's a given that you are planning to fail. Even though all the quotes about planning have been over-flogged, and the word's impact has been watered down; it still does not take away the profound truth of it. Every great business needs a great business plan.

At the sound of the need for a business plan, some would-be entrepreneurs may get distracted and overwhelmed about the details and what they could put in the business plan. But this is not something to be worried about. A business plan is basically your way of putting down the great business ideas in your head, and your solutions to those social, economic, or health problems you have identified in the marketplace. It is doing it in such a way that it is concise and understandable for the sake of clarity for anyone who looks at it. One more Bible verse may appeal to you on the topic of writing your business plan.

"Then the LORD answered me and said: "Write the vision and make it plain on tablets, that he may run who

reads it. For the vision is yet for an appointed time; but at the end it will speak, and it will not lie. Though it tarries, wait for it; because it will surely come, it will not tarry. Hab.2:2-3"

While it may take a lot of time, nothing beats a clear objective and plan spelt out in a document you can always go back to time after time. This is because anyone can have a great idea, and anyone can find a problem to solve, but what really separates the dreamers from the doers is the ability to turn those ideas into a viable business plan. As someone who has begun many start-up businesses, I can relate to the excitement of starting something new, especially if it is your brainchild or, as some people call it, 'the unicorn of their ideas.' I can relate to the adrenaline rush, the information overload, and –the best part- the overwhelming excitement to kick it off the ground and share it with the world.

But before you break out the office spaces, the capital, and form an LLC, you need to put your coordinated thoughts on paper. Make projections and estimations and find out what it will cost you for a start, then build on that information. This will help you stay focused and organized and know what to measure your future progress and advancement in the business with. In fact, some people have said that making a concise business plan increases your success in the business by 16 percent.

A good business plan functions as a test drive. It allows you to think about all the things you need to have in place to turn that brilliant idea into tangible business success and help you make the business run at its optimal performance. In the planning stages, you are even allowed to anticipate bumps or roadblocks or a sharp turn that might lie ahead in your entrepreneurial journey. These problems could be aggressive competitors, economic uncertainties, new technology and innovations, money issues, or maybe even yourself, the way your strengths and weaknesses could be an asset or liability in the face of conflict or crisis that may come out of your business endeavor. Your business plan also requires you to detail your costs, resources, and the appropriate timeline for the launch of your products and services.

As a business consultant, I have found one thing that is quite common among a lot of budding entrepreneurs who have come to share ideas about their start-up. When we get into it, and I ask them some questions about the planning of their business, you see the light of excitement in their eyes dim, and they are now more hesitant to explain more details of their business to you. An inevitable confusion starts to show entirely on their face, and then some of them carry slumped shoulders as if they are overwhelmed by all the things I have asked them to outline in their business plan. I have found out that nine out of ten times, this is because they are overwhelmed by the details, they have to go into in the business plan, and yes it gets overwhelming sometimes.

In this chapter, however, I will lay out a business plan's components to dispel all the myths and ambiguity surrounding it. But first, let us outline in detail why you need a business plan.

- **It is Actually Very Easy:** Once you get past the cloud of ambiguity surrounding the word 'business plan,' you should understand that it is just a written tool about your business that lays out your projections for the business for the next 3 to 5 years. It also outlines the path your business intends to take to generate revenue and clients. And when you break it down into mini plans like that, it loses its ability to intimidate you.

- **It Helps You Generate Realistic Milestones:** Any business plan that has been given a lot of careful thought helps you to take a step back and consider all your options, variables, and key business elements objectively. This is so that your decision-making is informed and helps you set achievable and feasible milestones. This, however, does not mean that your business plan will have all the answers; it just means that you are willing to anticipate the unknown while setting realistic goals.

- **It Helps You Steer Your Business As You Grow:** Your business plan acts as a sort of inbuilt GPS for your business. It helps guide you through every stage of development and management in your business. Your business plan also enables you to structure, run, and grow your business.

- **Gives You A Better Understanding of Your Customers:** For a business to succeed, you must have your hands on the pulse of things, and that is your customers. However, you cannot do this unless you have a great understanding of your clients' needs and who exactly they are and what your responsibility to them would be. Your business plan helps you determine those things you need to know about your clients. This is because an in-depth customer analysis is essential to an effective business plan and a successful business.

- **To Identify and Understand Your Competition:** I always tell my students that the ultimate test of a great business idea is that other people share it or want to buy into it. The truth is no one goes into business thinking about their competitors. Still, it is an essential factor you must put into consideration for the sake of your business success. A business plan allows you to identify and analyze your competition and decide your edge over them. It also helps you to understand their competitive advantages and determine what will make you stand out in the crowd.

- **To Assess the Feasibility of Your Venture:** The hallmark of every start-up is the ability to conduct research. For every factor included in your business consideration, you should research it and talk about it with consultants and experts. That is what your business plan affords you (the opportunity to assess that business venture's success or failure rate). This is important because more than it being something you are passionate about, it has to bring in revenue that exceeds the time, effort, and resources poured into it; else, it is just a hobby and not a business venture.

- **Determine Your Financial Needs:** How much would it take for your business to start up? Does it need capital? How much will you be able to invest in the business without going under? Do you need financial help from elsewhere? Your business plan helps you determine these questions and a lot more. How much capital you will need, and what you will use the money for. Your business plan should provide a detailed financial projection anywhere from three to five years ahead.

Components of a Business Plan

Now I can tell you with all certainty that no two business plans are ever the same. They come in different sizes, formats, and structures, but they all share a similar framework, and these can be presented in a particular order. The components that every business plan shares is what I have placed in the specific accepted order, so it is easy for anyone to choose from and build their own business plan.

- **Table of Content:** This is the guide to the important sections in your business plan, and it helps anyone reading it to navigate through the plan easily. You especially need this guide if your business plan is large or exceeds ten pages.

- **Executive Summary:** This summarizes your business plan's key points and draws the reader in at first glance. It outlines all the essential things anyone looking through the plan should see, and it should be able to capture the reader's attention in the first two sentences. That is why people employ copywriters to write the first part of their business plan with what is called a 'hook.' This is a sentence that captures and keeps the reader's attention for the whole of the read. It is most advised if your business plan is longer than ten pages.

- **Business Overview:** In this section, you describe your business and what you stand for as well as the nature of your business. This usually includes your company's vision and mission statement, values, products and services, and your company's unique selling points, plus what you plan to give to your clients. This basically tells us the purpose for the existence of your business.

- **Business Environment:** In this section, you include an analysis of your industry and the unforeseen forces at work in your market, things you or anybody else in the business has no power over. This also contains a description of your potential competitors; and a close look at your customers, what they want, who they are, and how they can access your products and services.

- **Marketing Plan:** Here is where you describe your brand. Your brand is basically you in relation to the business venture you want to undertake. You will also be required to outline your value proposition, plans on reaching prospective clients, make great sales, and develop a loyal clientele.

- **Financial Review:** In this section, you are required to include a detailed review of the state of your current finances and what you project they will look like in the nearest future. It typically contains financial statements, including an income statement, a tentative expenditure statement, and a revenue statement.

- **Action Plan:** This part of your business plan writing requires you to detail the steps you feel are involved in implementing your business plan. This usually includes the actual sequence of actions and how they align with your goals and objectives.

- **Appendices:** Finally, in this section, you can include detailed information that supports your business plan. These may be analyses, reports, surveys, legal documents, product specifications, and spreadsheets that deliver information that supports and empowers your business plan but which only your investors may ever read.

As I said before, there are no set-in-stone formats for your business plan, and so you are free to tailor yours to your business type and personality. These provided components are only here to guide you and inform you when writing your business plan. How you develop these parts is entirely up to you, there is still no format to writing them down. Just let your personality and the personality of your business shine through. There are, however, models tailor-made for every business type conceivable on the internet, and you could also use those to work on your business plan. The plan is to have fun drawing up your business plan, and if that isn't going as planned, you could involve the help of expert business strategists and consultants to help you draw it up. I remember that in late 2008 to early 2009, I used a template available on the internet to develop our business plan for Dominion Resources because we could not afford the services of a consultant or expert. Yet, in 2012, when the urge to approach lenders for business expansion came, we employed the services of an experienced consultant who crafted a more detailed and exhaustive plan for us for a fee. You can go that route too. In the fall of 2020, as I began to write a business plan for PLANET AVENUE, our new startup in e-commerce, it became evident that I needed an independent writer to assist me. I chose that approach because I needed someone to question my thinking faculty on the new venture and I, in return, could do a throwback asking why this or that concept among many choices. Excited yet? Get started writing that plan immediately! You are going to find out that there's so much energy and empowerment to be derived when you have your business plan written and ready.

CHAPTER 7

Finding your Funds

For a successful entrepreneur it can mean extreme wealth. But with extreme wealth comes extreme responsibility. And the responsibility for me is to invest in creating new businesses, create jobs, employ people, and to put money aside to tackle issues where we can make a difference.

Richard Branson, Founder Virgin Group

When I quit my job for the fortune 100 company I used to work with to start my own business, it was the great recession of 2008/2009. I was very vulnerable and exposed financially, but I knew it was time to go and start out on my own. In that single year, I had lived all the fears I had about leaving my job and beginning my own start-up. I had no investors, no previous pool of clients to rely on, and minimal resources placed in our banknotes. I know what it felt like to have nothing and no one and to venture out with only grit and determination as my backing. We were embarking on a franchise purchase worth several thousands of dollars. My wife and I had a decent amount of money in both of our workplace 401ks. As a financial advisor, I was in the business of counseling my clients against taking out their retirement savings prematurely because of the stiff penalties and truncation of their retirement goals.

I started this chapter with this because that is why many businesses are yet to kick off the ground despite their great business ideas; they have little or no ways of generating the capital the business needs. Many start-ups that also made the wrong moves on how they generated capital for their start-up business have folded. The truth is, for any capital-intensive business, one cannot do without a good source of funds.

When asked about their business funding, some of my students start talking a big game about investors and the hopes they place on them. This phenomenon I call "investor confidence." And when I then tell them the most acceptable ways, I feel one can generate the funds for their start-up, some of them look confused while the others insist on this 'easy' way of funding a business and wonder what I have against it. A couple of months -lugging your business plan around for potential investors to see- later, they begin to understand why I advised on the harder way.

This is because funding your business is one of the most important decisions you must make about your start-up. It is one of the most important financial decisions you will ever make in your life. How you choose to fund your business could affect how you structure your business, run it in the future, and even value your shares.

So, I had an intense conversation with my wife to win her approval to let us use our retirement savings at that point to plow into the business proposition in healthcare. I reminded her of our lifetime conversations with our children in 2005 and the opportunity to begin to fulfill our dreams to become entrepreneurs in America. She gave me a nod but insisted on seeing how that money would pay back, including the lost growth in trade off if we kept the money in our 401ks. I did my best to run growth comparisons between working 8-5 in big corporations and deciding our own future in our own business. The rest is history!

Now there are a lot of better ways to fund a start-up business, at least better than taking down your retirement savings, but before we go into that, I would take you through the reasons why your business does not need an investor.

- **You Don't Have Assets:** If you are just starting out in business and you are testing the proverbial waters, this means most times that you do not have assets, so in this case, it will be hard to get an investor interested in your business. To get outside funding for your business, you need to have assets to impress your potential investors, but if you can't yet show growth and a strong financial position, you have to have an impressive operation and management team or a definite and growing customer list, or a business idea so promising that investors are rushing to be a part of it. And with most start-ups, the case is they do not have these in their arsenal. Even the last one, a great business plan, is subjective. What one investor could see as impressive and promising; another investor could dismiss as a futile prayer.

- **Wasted Resources:** Now, another reason why finding investors is a bad idea for your start-up is the amount of money you could spend chasing after them. You have to learn about them and try to get into the places they can get into just to have access to them, and when you do, you might still face that rejection you are dreading. This is a harsh truth because people mostly do not care about you or your business. We are at the core of our being extremely selfish beings, and we want to get in on things that would benefit us, hence, the rat race to impress people you do not know so that they could help your business get off the ground. That money is of better use to you if diverted into your business.

- **Loss of Control:** Another hard truth people think they can handle about their start-ups till it happens is that when and if you eventually get investors to kick start your business, they may want to own an equity position in your business or have input in return for their money and for a business still in its inception, this could mean a change of direction for you and your business. Often, it is a direction that you would have no power over.

- **Loss of Accountability:** The success or failure of your business usually determines your attitude to it. By this, I mean that your business performance in the early years will determine how much you must invest in yourself and your time to make the business successful. Now, because you have already invited outsiders into your business who control your funds and decision-making, you may not feel the need to increase your performance.

By providing your own funds for your business, you have better control over your business and the profit it generates when it starts yielding fruit. And when you have total control, you are now better positioned to negotiate funding commitments to your company's advantage for people who want to get in on your business.

For the rest of this chapter, I want to show you **better ways to invest in your business without outside interference.**

- **Bootstrapping:** It is recorded that a third of all start-ups are funded by the owner or what we call bootstrapping. This is because when you want to start a business venture, the most obvious place to get the money for your business would be from your pockets or your savings. You can also get funds from your family and friends as a loan or a way to support your business. This is usually a very unconventional way of acquiring funds for your business start-up. This is easier because family and friends are generally more flexible when it comes to servicing your loan, much more than other external outlets.

    Now, the main advantage of self-funding or funding from friends is that you retain your business's sole ownership. Secondly, it helps you stay disciplined and focused on generating profits as it is in these profits that your business' chance for growth lies. Self-funding and funding from friends and family, however, cannot work for large-scale businesses. This is because the sole aim of any start-up that is self-funded is to generate profit so they can stay afloat instead of expanding. The result of this is that they sometimes miss big opportunities that otherwise well-funded businesses who have the financial flexibility will grab. In this way, they lose their chance to pursue innovations, new directions, or pivots in new business models. They also run the risk of tunnel vision as they do not have the opportunity of another person who has an invested interest in the business, giving them a new perspective to the business that would help them expand or grow.

- **Crowdfunding:** With the advent of modern technology and social media, the world now finds it easier to share its problems with the world on interactive social platforms. Crowdfunding platforms are set up for people to pitch their business ideas or challenges to a select public who are mostly investors or people willing to help you. This method only works for small businesses, where the pioneer of the business venture comes on the platform and shares a business idea along with his business model and its potential for growth. If the group members buy his ideas, they all make financial commitments to help him get the business off the ground. There are now many platforms like that for SMEs where every group member has a financial obligation to the group every month. This income is generated for the sole purpose of helping all their small businesses one after another.

  Crowdfunding helps create public interest for your business, somehow working as a free marketing strategy that also funds the business. It also eliminates the stress and consideration involved in sharing control of your business with an investor or a broker. Instead, your business belongs to you alone, and you only must report progress to people on the crowdfunding platform who cannot all have a share of your business. This also has the potential of attracting venture capital investment as the business progresses. However, one of the disadvantages of crowdfunding is the competition involved in pitching your idea to the audience if you are not the only one with the business idea in the group. You then have to focus on making your pitch solid enough to knock your competitors out of the water.

- **Venture Capital:** Venture capital funds are funds gotten from large corporations like retirement funds, school boards, and railway corporations. These funds are managed by professionals that have a keen eye for seeking out companies with great prospects. They are usually in a group, and they scout out solid start-up businesses and help them get on their feet. When these businesses gain an IPO, they move on to other businesses to partner with them too. Their money is not given to your business long term; the idea is to invest in the company's balance sheet and infrastructure until it reaches sufficient proportions and credibility before selling to a corporation or providing liquidation.

The main advantage of venture capital investment is that they monitor the growth and progress of the companies they invested in, thereby ensuring the sustainability and development of their investment. They also provide mentorship and guidance for the business owner that you don't have to pay for, and they help sustain your business growth effectively. However, they are only loyal to your business till they can recover their capital and profits from your business, and there is a time frame for this, which usually falls within 3 to 5 years. You also tend to lose control of a large part of your business to your venture capital investors. Venture capitalists can also invest in your competitors that are larger and more profitable. This could be a problem for your business as it may not be able to compete with all those other bigger companies.

You might not qualify for a venture capital consideration, but it helps to know inspirationally. You may determine to up the level of your new startup and decide to go all out to form a strong team with consultants and business investment experts working with you to prepare you for presentations and meetings with the investors. You can also decide to approach them later in the growth ladder of your business when you believe the time is right to scale your operations and enlarge your market.

- **Bank and Credit Card Loans:** In addition to getting money from family and friends, especially when you do not have enough saved up to start your business, one of the more acceptable ways to get funding for is through bank or credit card loans. Many banking institutions have a system set in place to provide loans to individuals who have a great business plan. This business plan must be superbly detailed, well-constructed, and structured to clearly convey the business sales strategy and profit forecast. These loans involve concise information of the valuation, along with the project report on which the loan was sanctioned. In this way, large capital can be gained by the entrepreneur who is seeking funding, and this could go a long way in fast-tracking the process of income generation. You also need huge collateral to start up this substantial business, and you might run a risk of losing that collateral if the business falls through or it takes more time to grow into its potential and start earning profits. These loans and the time to pay them back usually last about five to ten years, giving your business ample time to get off the ground and start earning the returns it needs to pay back the loan. One way to qualify for a bank loan from the early stages of your entrepreneurial journey is to cultivate a solid relationship with your banker.

I will recommend writing a powerful business plan detailing your vision and mission, as well as defining the need your product or service is going to meet in the market. Show your banker that you are not going to lose money, rather, you are going to create value which will turn to sustainable growth and profits in the years to come. You must indeed, work arduously to protect your credit because all loans are based on the faith and credit of the business owner. Inevitably, your credit score and reports make or mar your ability to qualify for a credit card approval or bank loan. It is just that definite in America. A poor credit status may reveal your carelessness and untrustworthiness in carrying out your business operations and the lenders want assurances that they would get their money back with interests. We decided early on to fight tooth and nail to keep our credit at high marks and it has continued to pay off for us.

CHAPTER 8

Building your Team early

Great things in business are never done by one person, they're done by a team of people

Steve Jobs, Founder/CEO, Apple

The minute you get up and get concerned about the things happening around you so much that it births a business idea, and you take responsibility for this business idea and decide to nurture it to success, you are ready to become a leader. In fact, the whole process of getting the idea and harnessing it, and then stepping out to run with it has already shown leadership traits and signs of excellent business leadership. That, in essence, is what being your own boss is. And to make you a more effective and better leader, you must find the right people to hire and delegate efficiently.

When a lot of people hear about delegation in a small business setting, they get irritated for many reasons that they have told me, or I have deduced. They are either terrified or unsure of or overwhelmed with the prospect of trusting someone else to run parts of the business they have taken so much time and energy to put together. For this set of people, I sort of understand them, and I can totally relate to why they do not want to entrust their brainchild into the hands of someone else. And then the second group of people gets so flustered with the idea of the amount of time it would take to train new people in this new business and then trust them with those time-consuming tasks. Another category of people I have come across is the group that cannot trust others to be honest and trustworthy in their roles. Some of these are borne out of experience or what they hear from others.

While going through a book by Fred Halstead, "Leadership Skills that Inspire Incredible Results," it drove home the sad truth about the number of businesses that have failed or remained stagnant because the owners have refused to delegate their tasks effectively. From my experience and from short surveys I have given some of my protégés, I have put together some strong reasons why people find it difficult to delegate in their new business.

- **The 'Only I Can Do It' Mindset:** As I've said before, starting a business is scary, and you are pouring in everything about you into that venture and starting it so much that it sometimes becomes your life. But I hate to break it to many people; entrepreneurship requires a lot more skills than just finding the solution to a problem. With the advent of social media and digital marketing, there are now so many ways to push your business and make things run smoothly for you, and you need people who are skilled in all those aspects to help you run your business smoothly. Even if by some stroke of genius, you manage to learn all those skills by yourself, the amount of time it would take you to complete those tasks by yourself is the same time you could have spent trying to find more innovative ways to expand your business. To understand how vital your role is as your business leader, you must understand the difference between working in the business and working on the business. Your job is to work on the venture, look at it from a creator's perspective, tweak it, and find ways to make it better, instead of working in the business where you waste more time doing tasks outside of your skillset or comfort zone.

- **Feeling There's No Time For Delegation:** I find this reason very hilarious, but it actually happens. I have seen entrepreneurs approach me with complaints when it comes to delegation. "They just don't get it!" "They have been with me for so long, and don't know how to do so and so by themselves. Do I have to do everything by myself?" These are just a few of the frustrating complaints that some of my start-up entrepreneurs come to me with. And while I empathize with them greatly, I cannot relate to their problem. No matter how long a person has stayed with you, no matter how loyal or dedicated they are, they cannot read your mind. You may have the solution to a problem and how you want it solved, but you cannot do it all. One of the reasons for the untimely extinction of many one-man businesses is exactly because the owners "don't have the time to delegate". Rather, they continue to run the show until there is nothing to run.

- **Lack of Trust:** In every start-up business, there must be people who you know have caught your vision and can run with it. True enough, your trust should be earned by them, but you should be willing to trust them with your ideas and parts of your business. This is very hard for many entrepreneurs to do; they are so paranoid that they treat every one of their employees with aloofness or downright hostility. Thinking that people can steal your ideas or your clients or that they may have ulterior motives when it comes to your business is an entirely valid fear. However, not everyone is out to steal your business ideas and your clients. When you learn that loyalty is earned, too, it will go a long way in making your relationship with your employees smoother. Learn to delegate your duties in bits to your staff members who have a record of honesty, competency and who have the requisite skills, experience, and motivation. You will find out that your business will be more productive.

- **Lack of Confidence:** One of the most unpopular reasons some entrepreneurs do not delegate their duties is that they have no confidence or belief in the business's future direction. They do not want to step out and embarrass themselves if it does not work out. In another sense, they know the direction of their business, but they do not have the confidence to explain the why and how of it all to the people they are leading. They then project their frustration and insecurity on their staff and magnify their flaws instead of their own fears. This not only wins you the trust and loyalty of your employees but also fosters unproductiveness in their workplace. This problem can easily be solved by sitting down with your staff and advisors and listening carefully to all the input and arguments they present. This not only gives you clarity about what they want to be able to flourish and succeed in your workplace, but it will also provide you with insight into the possible directions your business could take for the growth and development of your company.

- **The Fear of Losing Control:** The terms 'micromanager' and 'control freak' are not nice or flattering terms when used in a relationship with anyone, especially in a business setting. Many people are terrified of delegating because the people they delegate to may steal their business or take over control of operations. They feel like they are handing over the reins of the venture and running it to their employees if they give them the sort of power that delegation gives them. The truth most people do not see in this situation is that the reins of the business always belong to you; no one knows your vision or passion more than you do, so giving them control of some parts of the business doesn't mean they can take over from you or sabotage you. You will always be the founder and pioneer of your business; you will always be the one who makes the final decisions concerning any matter, so your fear, in essence, is unfounded. Truth be told, some unscrupulous employees have undermined their employers, but it always comes down to the kind of person you are as an entrepreneur. If you are alive and able, if your employees disappoint you in a way that humbles you, yes, grieve over it but don't let it kill you or your business. Dust up your business plan and reclaim your authority. Hire new people, offer training to those who remain with you and lift them up. Boost morale and think of new and innovative ways to relaunch and start over. As the saying goes, "It is never over until it is over."

Nothing beats having a group of people who have bought your trust with their loyalty. And nothing is more fulfilling than training your people by yourself. Many people think the time used to teach people is a waste as we are a very unreliable species; we change with the wind and what the day brings. We forget that our customers are the same way too; the fickleness of human nature does not only apply to our employees and customers. I still maintain that the best investment you will ever make is in the people around you.

For the rest of this chapter, though, I will outline **simple ways to build your team and delegate work efficiently.**

- **Genuinely caring about people will make them more interested in working for and with you for your business success.** Anyone who understands that you have their best interest at heart and are interested in their growth will blossom under that care and give you their support and loyalty without coercion.

- **Knowing the strength and weaknesses of your team also helps you delegate to them very effectively.** This will also help you place realistic expectations on them and the task you give them.

- **Learn to be more interested in the outcome than in the process.** It is essential to know the difference between supervision and micro-managing. Be more interested in telling them the expected result and not the process. Trust them to do the work you have assigned to them. Also, be truly clear and concise about the outcome and the deadline of the task you have given.

- **Do not delegate too late.** Many people wait till they are burnt out and overwhelmed by work before they start looking for people to outsource the work to and then expect them to perform magic or do the impossible. Learn to be proactive in your delegation.

- **Train your team!** There is no amount of time you spend training your team that is a waste of your time or resources. You do not gain anything by being the only person who knows how to do anything. It will benefit you more if other people in your team know how to do those tasks, too, so that your work does not just grind to a halt in the incidence of your absence.

CHAPTER 9

The Power of Good Mentorship

One of the greatest values of mentors is the ability to see ahead what others cannot see and to help them navigate a course to their destination.

John Maxwell, American Author, Speaker & Pastor

As with having a team that has your back, every entrepreneur needs a mentor who will guide you through the process. It took me a lot of time to understand and let this thought sink in that I did not have to walk this path alone. Even a sole proprietor needs someone to rely on for guidance. Over time, the word mentorship has gone through a lot of changes that it seems even the meaning has been corrupted or gone through some sort of evolution. And with this evolution, there appears to be a lot of negative emotions and misconceptions attached to it, so many people have become leery of the word and have developed an acquired disdain for the institute of mentorship.

I will digress a little, but for the sake of more clarity and more understanding, I would explore the history of mentorship slightly as it were. It has been recorded that the first mention of the concept started with the character of Mentor in Homer's Odyssey. Around the time in ancient Greek, Odysseus entrusted his son Telemachus into the hands of his trusted friend and companion Mentor before he went on to fight in the Trojan war. As the legend goes, he was away for a long time, and in that time, Mentor nurtured and taught the boy in the ways of warriors and men, and he grew up to be a fine young man.

In 2007, Mckim, Jollie, and Hatter made a historical link between the word "mentorship" and the middle ages explaining that mentoring became common practice in the time of the guilds and trade apprenticeships when young men, having acquired some technical skills, often benefited from the patronage of more experienced and established professionals.

In the 1970s, businesspeople and researchers started to recognize the vital role of mentors in corporate executives' development. Since then, it has been used increasingly in the workplace to help a junior colleague or member of staff progress.

There have been arguments going around for a while about the need (or lack of it) of mentors for entrepreneurs stating that mentors' role is overrated and that a lot of budding entrepreneurs have survived and succeeded without mentorship. In fact, many of these entrepreneurs do not seek out mentorship with the urgency and effort they put into seeking out partners and investors.

I believe that results speak for themselves, and from what has been passed down through history, a lot of big businesses around the world with great names like Facebook, Apple, and Google had founders who had mentors. You should not find it new that Steve Jobs of Apple Inc. was mentored by a guy named Mike Markkula. Jobs went on to mentor Facebook's Mark Zuckerberg. Also, Larry Page and Sergey Brin of Google were mentored by Eric Schmidt. This shows you how important these big names thought mentorship was, and they invested in those mentorship relationships.

When I started out as an entrepreneur myself, I was fortunate to enjoy a solid mentorship. Mine was made easy by reason of an initial franchisee-franchisor relationship. Even when the franchise was pulled, the owners continued to avail us unimaginable support. A wiseman has said that "Only a fool would like to experiment on every idea!" In other words, you do not have to do it alone, you can enjoy the help of those ahead of you to show you the ropes and share their mistakes so that you do not have to fall into the error lane all the time. This mantra was central to my intentional approach to seeking mentor advice at the initial stages of our business. I have found out along the way that you never end needing guidance even when you think you have achieved success of your own or built experience of entrepreneurship. I have also invested in books and online courses and studied other men who had been successful in the business I had ventured into. My friends often look at me in amazement how I speak freely about Warren Buffett of Berkshire Hathaway, Bill Gates of Microsoft, and Jeff Bezos of Amazon as if I have lunch with them often. No, I don't have the privilege of lunching with them, but I have spent considerable time learning how they run their organizations and what I could glean from each of them. I found out that despite being the world's richest man for many years, Bill Gates had turned to Warren Buffet for intentional mentorship. I realized that Mr. Buffett's annual letter to the shareholders of Berkshire Hathaway is a highly sought-after guide to investing and corporate leadership. Mr. Williams (Bill) Gate is an avid reader and annually recommends books to his followers. He motivated me to invest in "Blinkist", the condensed books app that allows you to read or listen to summaries of many business books on your gadget. I can say with all reasonableness, that I attribute my foray into e-commerce in 2020, during the global COVID-19 Pandemic, to listening to several books on entrepreneurship on Blinkist. I listen to Blinkist when I am doing my daily 3-mile walk or on the treadmill. I listen when I am in the shower and any time it is convenient. In other words, you can gain mentorship through books.

I also found out that Mr. Jeff Bezos has been largely successful because he placed a lot of emphasis on organizational leadership with lots of men and women at the helm of affairs. Not only that, he believes in process management, a high necessity for an unparalleled success in e-commerce and distribution logistics, the type we have never heard of in the retail world until his emergence.

The flexibility of mentorship, which was not there in the past, has shown that the most crucial ingredient in your relationship with a mentor is communication, as with other relationships. And that communication can now be carried out over a lot of platforms; there could be face-to-face meetings, there could be online interaction through many platforms. And what is even more interesting, your mentor could also be a member of your family. Mentorship could also be casual or structured formally, depending on the involved parties' personality and disposition. I follow Mr. Bill Gates on LinkedIn and all his very inspiring and educational posts are dropped into my feed daily so I can learn the next new thing he has to offer.

For the rest of this chapter, I would outline **the importance and benefits of mentorship as a start-up business** in clear detail.

- **You Gain A Life's Worth of Experiences:** One of the things that shape a man or woman is his/her experiences, and there is only so much about a man's experiences that you can glean from books. In the business and corporate world, experience is gold. It is the lack of expertise that births so much trial and error, rookie mistakes that many new entrepreneurs make. When you gain access to an experienced person's life, it saves you a lot of mistakes and sets you on the path of the success they have experienced or even more.

- **It Increases Your Chances of Success:** Your chances of success in life and business can be greatly multiplied by having the right mentor. A survey conducted in 2013 stated that about 80 percent of the entrepreneurs and CEOs said they received some sort of mentorship for their business. Another study conducted by Sage also showed that 93 percent of the start-ups attested to mentorship, which was instrumental to their success. A mentor brings so much to the table for any young entrepreneur. They bring their connections, experiences, failures, knowledge, and a whole lot more that will catapult you to greatness if utilized well.

- **You Have Access To Their Network:** Every successful man or woman in business has an invaluable personnel resource at their disposal, and getting access to such men who are now invested in your growth and your business's growth, will enable you to gain access to that resource. These resources could even include investors or partners who can help you get ahead. And just by being in the company of this person and being a part of his or her network, it has already provided you free publicity and visibility that you would never have had if you did not have a mentor.

- **A Mentor Gives You Longevity**: A lot of new businesses that folded in their inception are an abysmal number. And all these businesses may have made it had they had the guidance of a mentor with experience in their field. A mentor helps your business survive longer in the market.

- **They Help You Develop a Great EQ:** One of the popular ways to run your business to the ground is to mix it up with emotions or let your emotional connections mess with your judgment. One of the advantages of a mentor is that they help you see things that you do not see when your emotions are running high or low, and they help you get those errant emotions under control. They help show you how to behave and react to certain circumstances and situations. And then they encourage you to do and be better. You will probably see a lot of setbacks and obstacles in your business, and only a few men who do not have the encouragement and backing of a mentor scale through those conditions and still succeed in their business.

I cannot recommend this too much. All I know is that Dominion Cares has achieved a modest success because we lean on our mentors all the time. If you operate in a highly regulated industry like home care where we are, you cannot do it alone; you always need to run to your mentor for advice and guidance. It is often said that "If you want to go fast, go alone; if you want to go far, go in the company of others." I will say, if you want to grow and go far, go on the shoulders of your mentors. As it always turns out, over time, your mentor also defers to you with one or two questions to show that you too have gained their trust and respect.

What if you do not have a definite person to call a mentor? There are many resources out there to help you gain access. You can join the Chamber of Commerce of your city and any other business-related community where you can deliberately associate with a leader and warm up to them for assistance. You can also look up such resources online, say on LinkedIn or Facebook groups. It can also be in your religious organization or church. Let them know who you are, what you do, and how they can be of value to help you grow. You will face rejection and snobbery but do not give up because at the end, you will find someone out there to help and assist you in your journey to success.

PART 3

THE ACHIEVEMENTS OF AN ORGANIZATION ARE
THE RESULTS OF THE COMBINED
EFFORT OF EACH INDIVIDUAL.

Vinve Lombardi,
American, & National Football League (NFL) Executive

CHAPTER 10

The Power of Organization

Outstanding leaders go out of their way to boost the self-esteem of their personnel. If people believe in themselves, it's amazing what they can accomplish."
Sam Walton, Founder of Walmart and Sam's Club

Let us say you walk into a food court with all the restaurants setting up stands and selling take out. You are probably with some friends and you just want to have a good meal and some fun along with it. You and your friends walk past the first stand and it's like the picture of chaos, people are standing by the counter complaining about their order and how late it was, the waiters or servers are busy yelling at each other and at the customer and the manager is somewhere in the background looking lost and overwhelmed in turns. Then you walk past the second stand and the waiters are wearing very welcoming smiles while serving the food and there are no customers complaining about the customer service or the quality of their food.

At this point I do not have to ask you which stand or restaurant you would order your food from. Even if the first restaurant had better food, you would choose the one that looked better over the chaotic stand. And this is true for everyone. The fundamental truth of the matter is that people respond to and are drawn to order. The world is already noisy and chaotic enough, we just want to snatch up little bits of calm wherever we can, and shitty service and chaos would not just cut it.

Yet, I am sure that everyone has at least had an experience with those kinds of businesses. It may not be a restaurant, it may be an online store, or a firm. But we have seen the evidence of a lack of organization in several business establishments and you probably left the place vowing never to use their services ever again. This also applies to firms and corporations. Every business is unique in its operations, visions, and services, but the basic structure of any business is the same such that you can smell the disharmony and lack of structure from a mile away.

For the sake of the success of the business, every business owner must be a lot of things at once. And they must be able to perform all those tasks effectively and efficiently to ensure the smooth running of their business. Therefore organization, also known as structure, is an especially important part of business operations. This is why entrepreneurs hire planners, assistants, and more staff in general so that things run more smoothly, and their customers and employees are happy. Good organizational skills have the power to make or break a business; it could also mean the difference between a fulfilled workday and a stressful one.

There is however a sort of disorganization curse that plagues every small business, and this seems to happen for a lot of reasons. One of the reasons is that the business is in infancy and everyone is still learning their roles and their place in the workspace, including the owner of the business himself. If the disorganization stems from this, I call it the 'growing pains phenomenon.' This kind of disorganization is relatable and can be turned around immediately the employees and everyone in the firm learn their synergy and get comfortable in their own skin in the business. As the trust and the communications flow, the synergy flows with it and the disorganization is blown out of the water.

The second reason is that small businesses are usually always strapped for cash and may not be able to afford new employees or the resources it would take to bring in more facilities that would make their businesses more organized. I am talking about automation, the application of technology and communication tools to help organize the business. The third reason is usually the chaos in the life of the entrepreneur that is bleeding into their business. Your brand is you more than it is your business, and that is why entrepreneurs must go through training to learn emotional intelligence, human relations, and a host of other things. This is because if there is chaos in your own life, you could not teach anyone about organization if you tried hard. It is a life principle; you cannot give what you do not have, and this sets your business up for failure before you even give it a chance to succeed.

Now even though hiring enough staff and designation of tasks properly is a great way to organize your company's operations, it is not the only way to make your company organized and a lot of people do not know that. I once had someone ask me in a hall full of entrepreneurs, saying "My business is really small, but I have enough staff and the work is going smoothly, why then does it feel like there's still no synergy among my workers?"

The answer to this is simple: organization starts first as a physical exercise before it becomes mental. If your office spaces are not organized and maximized, there is no need hiring a million people. Productivity will still be on a low because your immediate environment is fostering chaos and like it or not, it affects their psyche and their productivity more than you know.

Here are a few ways to organize your office environment to foster maximum productivity in your business:

- **Tame Your Office Space:** Nothing speaks disorganization more than an office where nothing has a specific place. Documents are everywhere and not properly filed; you must upend the whole place to find a tax review document or a shareholder agreement. This can be hard. Paper is one of the most populous commodities in many offices and if not filed correctly, it makes your offices look like a tornado just passed through. Get a better filing system and pull all those documents in a file room where you can get access to it easily. Even better, go paperless. There are so many software apps and tools that you could use to organize your books and print them out only when you need a hard copy. It saves up space for you and makes the place look better for your customers and employees.

- **Make Your Customers Happy:** Without customers, you might as well just close shop and go home. They are the heart and soul of your business, so making them happy should be your priority. There are many tools now that make it easy to keep track of your loyal customers, manage their tickets effectively and make it easier for your employees to interact with them favorably. This frees up more time for you to concentrate on improving your products and services. Be careful though not to automate the whole process as it may take away the personal touch and defeat its main purpose.

- **Manage Your Expense Receipts:** One thing I have found very frustrating while running a small business is the managing of expense reports. It takes a lot of time and effort to track and record them in time for taxes. I started using an automated system that helps track it and it helped me do a lot of the work. There are apps like QuickBooks, Rydoo, Expensify, ZohoExpense and a lot of others. You just must find one that is a good fit with your business and you are good to go. I have found QuickBooks to be adequate for our operations from day 1. We have grown from the basic payroll app to the enhanced payroll. Also, we are now at the Enterprise level of QuickBooks with dedicated customer service called "Priority Circle" with ability to get a call back within 5 minutes of initiating a support request, among other benefits. We got there in over ten years. Start from where your need is - number of employees, customer count and revenue levels.

- **Keep Track of Your Passwords:** A lot of people have this system in their office of using one password for everything that requires an account and a password. That seems effective at first, but then this just makes your accounts easy to target and attack if someone were to try. Some other people with a healthy dose of paranoia do not actually use one password, they use several that they do not always remember and then rely on being able to reset them if they need to. This is not only irresponsible; it makes work more tedious than it must be. Now, tedious work makes for more time wasted and since time is money, anything costing you more time to manage than they are worth, is invariably costing you much needed revenue. Apart from using Apple iOS or Google or Samsung Password save and auto-refill feature, you can get a password saving app or program like 1password to help you keep your passwords organized and accessible.

- **Improve Your Workspace Aesthetics:** Like I said before, a good workspace enables creativity and productivity and the way your offices are designed goes a long way in doing that. Invest in making your offices look more habitable, friendly, and professional. It may be potted plants or potpourri that you need to spice up the place; it may be a sound system playing soft music, and it could even be a redoing of your walls with ambient colors that are great and soothing. You could get an interior decorator to have these things done for your offices and it will show in the general results of your company.

There are a lot of other ways to make your offices look professional and create order in your business, but then since it is an inclusive task, maybe you need to sit down with your employees or an expert to decide how to improve your workspace and make you more organized. This could be the dividing line between you and another startup that makes you look more professional and more successful.

CHAPTER 11

The Irreplaceable Power of Successful Public Relations

People do not buy goods and services. They buy relations, stories and magic.

Seth Godin, Author & Entrepreneur

If you have followed me on this journey from chapter one, you must have heard me say more than once that the wealth you seek, and your business needs are in people. If there were no customers or clients to patronize your business, you might as well just close the shop and go home. Then if you are thinking about generating lasting wealth for your children and their children after that, then the responsibility of your business and everyone in there is to invest in relationships with people.

Some people might still find the term "Public Relations" or "PR" ambiguous or vague; they are not sure if its meaning is literal or otherwise. Many people have a vague understanding of what it means. Some think that it is a term largely associated only with public figures and celebrities. PR happened to be one of my beloved majors in my first degree and so, I can explain what it means knowledgeably.

Public Relations is the deliberate control of the release of information and communication between a company and its public, in a way that is mutually beneficial to both parties. It could include an organization or company gaining

exposure to their public audience through topics of public interest and news items that do not require direct payment. Personally, I call it the business of controlling the narrative and getting it out to the audiences that matter to you and your organization. It extends to how you want the world to perceive your brand, product, or service, including your personae. To that extent, some consider PR as Image or Reputation Building. Some organizations carve out functions for PR or Community Relations usually under a Marketing departmental structure.

As a startup business, one of your major goals and points of focus should be on building your brand and reputation and making it as visible as you can manage. There is no better way to do this than by employing and investing in marketing strategies. One of the most effective and cost-effective marketing strategies, however, is public relations! Here, you are proactive, and you control the way the public sees you and the brand you are building. A lot of people think it is not worth the amount of money you invest into controlling your narrative. Some will argue that there are better marketing strategies that you could use to brand your business positively and gain publicity like referral programs and magazine features. It amuses me to no end when people say things like that around me. What they do not know is that those strategies are also public relations at work. I mean, it is basically building and controlling the narrative for your company in such a way that it benefits you and your public positively. You can therefore say that Public Relations is marketing, if not all of it.

Effective Public Relations helps to create awareness and allows for you to control the way in which your company is perceived by customers, media, and the industry at large. If this is done the right way, this awareness and publicity will turn into trust and confidence in your business. This in turn turns into quantifiable lead generation, success, and profit. One of the big advantages of a good PR program is the potential to attract job seekers because everybody believes you are running a great organization worthy of their time and skills. A lot of entrepreneurs, however, do not appreciate the importance of PR or make it a priority early. In an ideal setting, every startup should start building good relationships with influencers and the media. It is an investment that will guarantee long lasting success and sustainable wealth.

The foundation of a good public relations strategy is your story. Since your story is your brand and your brand is your first representation to the world as an entrepreneur, you need to sit down and decide what that story should be. What does your company stand for, and how do you plan to play it to the public? Ask yourself questions like; "Why am I in this business?" "What do I offer?" "What makes my organization unique?" "What are my unique selling points?" "What gives me an edge over my competition?" I call this defining your individuality in business. This is the hardest part of the process, but when you get this out of the way, you are already set to go.

As you are going through this process, learn to treat anyone who can help you like a partner. This gesture will only seem genuine if you truly develop an interest in them. Get to know them on a more personal level. Everyone loves to be seen and appreciated, and anyone you give this would be loyal to you. Build a solid network with key people who are instrumental to your growth and that of your business. This will take time, but its rewards far outweigh its cost. These people could be reporters, social media experts, bloggers, radio and TV presenters, YouTubers, or just anyone with an audience and a voice. They could be instrumental in getting you the credibility and exposure that your business will thrive on.

Anyone could talk themselves blue in the face trying to convince an entrepreneur that PR is necessary for their company's growth and they still would not believe them. So, I will take the time to list out the importance and benefits of good public relations strategies for your business.

- **It Helps Manage Your Company's Reputation:** Most people always think of PR as what you do to control damages after a bad stunt goes down that has the power to take your company under. It is not a falsehood or bad karma to acknowledge that things could go wrong in your company and you would need PR to salvage the situation. But first off, you need to take a proactive role in the way your company and business is viewed by the public. You do not have to wait for those unfavorable conditions to come; get on the offensive. And you can start this by building strong connections with the media organizations in your community. This way, when those crises come up, you can start to repair them simply by a press release or an interview that enables you to correctly present your story. This solution will not be possible if you do not invest in good PR from the beginning.

- **It Helps Promote Brand Values:** One of the major intangibles you sell as a business owner is trust and confidence in your brand and what it stands for. One of the best ways to adequately accomplish this is to increase your credibility by improving your reputation through thought leadership pieces, networking strategies and connections with influencers. Building trust between you and your clients may determine if your business floats or sinks. It could also determine your company's staying power in the face of crisis. With the help of good PR, you could send positive messages to your customers and your public by using positive topics that they are responsive to.

- **It Enhances Your Online Presence:** In a world where digital and online presence is now the new cool, good PR could help you stay ahead of the curve in your business by making the most of your online presence. With the help of social media and the press, you can choose the way your business is represented, and which platforms work best for you. In the occasion of new products and services, you would not need to spend so much money marketing this new product if your company already has good PR. You will only ride on the reputation you have already built to make your new product as popular as the ones before. Because then it is not just the product that you are selling, you are also selling your brand along with the trust you have built with it.

- **It Helps Strengthen Community Relations:** The community is made up of your customers, potential customers, job seekers as well as decision makers around you. These blocks constitute your target audience. When you invest in good public relations strategies and connect with them by fighting causes that they are passionate about, or through charity donations or scholarships, you show them that you are part of the local market and you are interested in building and maintaining ties with them. These ties would prove extremely useful in the years to come, either for you or for your children. And that is how many companies build lasting wealth for their generations to come.

- **Public Relations Helps You Stay Ahead of the Competition:** Good PR helps you gain not just an inside but outside view of your business and strategies. Because good communication is not one-sided, you can talk to your audience and get a response from them in return. You communicate by establishing your brand identity and getting the public to see you for what you are and the service you are providing. You can engage with them through social media by organizing charities, or live videos or live seminars. You can get the needed feedback on those PR strategies you used on those platforms in the form of surveys, comments, and blog posts. Then you can know which business strategies or products work best for your public and better tailor them to their taste. Any business that can do this will always have an edge over their competitors.

CHAPTER 12

Building generational wealth, the unrivaled glory of business owners

Building wealth is a marathon, not a sprint. Discipline is key ingredient.

Dave Ramsey,
Popular Finance Advisor, Radio show host, Author, & Businessman

Ask a business owner to name the top five reasons why they are in business; I bet 99.9% of the time they will communicate the desire to transfer inheritances to their children and generations after them. Other answers would include building their retirement nest egg, and the independence to make their own determinations rather than the usual 8-to-5-day job that only helps other people to achieve their dreams.

The question is, if everyone is in business for their legacies, how do they do it? What are the best practices to go about achieving this issue of establishing financial posterity in your family and community?

Ideas diverge but here are some critical steps to turning your business to a wealth building entity beyond just paying your staff and

yourself salaries and offering benefits as needed:

1. **Define your wealth generation goals:** You may not be able to put a dollar amount on this, but you can have a ballpark of goals. How many children do you have and if they are already building their families, how many grandchildren are there? What is your idea of leaving them an inheritance? What do you want to be remembered for in your community? Do you want to be known as supporting good causes like education, entrepreneurial development, the arts, or solving problems?

2. **Conscious devotion to watching the "machines" of your business:** By this I mean paying attention to your bottom line on a regular basis, avoiding over-leveraging your finances, making sure your staff are at the best they can be and are driven to achieve success for themselves and for you. How do you handle your inventories, billing, and collection? Do you have the capacity to handle all the demands of your day-to-day operations, from HR to Production, to Finance, to Marketing, and Administration? A weakness or vacuum in any of these important areas may begin to tell on your ability to meet your financial needs, not to talk of building a reserve for tomorrow.

3. **What is Your Endgame and Exit Strategy?** If you ask many business owners what their end game is, they stammer in their response. Many will say it the way they see it, "I don't know!" There are usually two types of exit strategy – sell your company or transfer it to your heirs. Early in my entrepreneurial adventure, I determined to build my company to a place where I would be able to sell and cash out at a good price. I would need the proceeds for my retirement and then, for legacy building and wealth transfer. Do you want to sell your business at a good price and at the right time? Or you plan to transfer it to your heirs, that is, if you are lucky to have anyone among your children who is interested in running and taking over your business in your twilight years?

4.   **Keep your eyes on the legal and compliance requirements of your industry:** Many business owners soon go burst because of running afoul of the law or failing to meet the regulatory benchmarks of their sector. These can happen through careless HR issues, forgetting to submit paperwork as required by national, state, or local governments. One year I forgot to submit an annual liability insurance renewal paper to the Department of Human Services. Six months down the road, the hammer came down hard on our company. Our biweekly reimbursement bills running into several thousands of dollars were cut off. I was distrustful and humbled, not because we did not renew our insurance, but I failed to send the paperwork to the government office where it should go as proof of meeting the requirement for keeping our license current. How about the annual renewal of your business registration with your Secretary of State? Imagine going to the bank to discuss a loan application and your banker tells you, Sir, I found out that your business has been inactive for several months! That could be a red flag to a loan officer that you could be a bad manager of their funds. One advice my mentor said out loud to me and my wife was to avoid owing the Internal Revenue Service (IRS) at all cost. She added that the IRS is your #1 Employee, and you cannot afford to not pay your #1 Employee! Well, between 2010 – 2011 we raked up a deficit of $42500 in our withholding deposits to the IRS. By 2012, we received an unannounced visitor in our office from the local IRS office and made it known that she had the power to take us out of business unless we arrange to pay the debts back. To the good credit of our CPA, we entered a deal that allowed us to pay the money back by monthly installments. By the end of 2016 when we paid it all up, we must have paid over $100,000. Imagine what that could have hampered our wealth generation goals. Several years ago, a businessman was owing the IRS close to half a million dollars in taxes. He flew his private jet into the IRS building in Houston, Texas to "end it all." Imagine what that meant to his wealth building and transfer to his children![1]

5. **Learn from the Masters:** There are known families that have built their businesses over several generations and are still thriving. The largest employer of labor in America, Walmart, was founded by Sam Walton when he opened his first retail store in Arkansas in 1962. When he died in 1992, he safely transferred his fortunes to his five children. Three of the Forbes 2020 World Billionaires – Alice Walton, Jim Walton, and Rob Walton – are heirs of Mr. Sam Walton with individual wealth of $61.3billion. These three are numbers 17, 18 and 19 of the 2020 richest people on earth.[2] Study a few of the names on the list and what makes them tick year in, year out. I follow the top names in the list, from Bill Gates to Elon Musk, to Jeff Bezos and Warren Buffet. I am not crazy about becoming like them, but I show interest in their work and the benevolences they carry out to help poor communities around the world. I would like to create lasting legacies through my entrepreneurial activities. I would like to bequeath to my heirs my wealth and activities that help the less privileged.

6. **Fight to keep your boat tight and secure:** One of the things that could mess up your legacy and wealth bequeathing goals is racking up debts such as through bank loans or credit cards. If care is not taken, you may see the bottom fall off your business which, from all intent and purpose, you have spent the best of your active years to build. One of the things I hate is to see high interest charges on our bank's cash flow line of credit due to high balances. I hate high credit card balances and the interest rate they accrue. You are invariably giving away the wealth you are building to strangers. Sometimes I see the credit system as vulturous and carnivorous; institutions profiting from your sweat. But then, you created the possibility of that ever happening by your lifestyle. In this contest therefore, "fighting" means keeping a manageable financial exposure and constantly paying your debts as needed. The credit monitoring agencies will tell you to never miss even a month of payment or forfeiting your

account to collection agencies who have no mercies in rendering your credit life worthless. PAY YOUR DEBTS and if possible, avoid them! They keep you miles away from achieving your financial dreams, legacy building, and wealth transfer!

7. **Keep your employees at a high interest level and energy:** As I have said before in some pages, your employees are your most important assets you can ever parade to have. Create ways to always keep their energy and interest in your company high. Things happen, employees come and go (because they are not owners of the business) but create environments that enable them to contribute their best to the success of your company. Because I have been there, I know the pain of constantly losing staff and going through an unending cycle of rehiring and retraining people. In the process, you lose the needed momentum in your market, your customers begin to see you as unreliable and weak, especially if they are having to deal with different people in your organization on a regular basis. As they say, hire people who are smarter than you and more knowledgeable. If you cannot find them, make the best of the people you can hire by growing them to your best through training, workplace benefits and competitive remunerations. Sometimes I wonder if keeping good people is by luck or answer to prayer! They are, but also by your conduct, actions, honesty, and trustworthiness.

8. **Seek opportunities for growing your wealth:** One of the quotes extensively used in money talks is Mr. Warren Buffet's saying that "If you don't find a way to make money while you sleep, you will work until you die!" He also said that "Opportunities come infrequently. When it rains gold, put out the bucket, not the thimble." I see the stock market as an avenue for a business owner to build wealth. Some stocks and mutual funds earn annual returns far greater than the banks can ever pay you in interest on your deposits or certificates. Through the

power of compounding, your investment's returns in annualized growth and dividends reinvestment, can grow to the place where you want to comfortably say you can give to your heirs. Your business should therefore be a springboard to your wealth creation, not the end of it. Ask yourself, how are the billionaires doing it? For some of them, it is through their stakes in their corporations, but most of them it is because they retain investment managers who invest their money for them and keep the wealth creation wheels moving time and time. You can start by a DIY approach to investing in the stock market, or by working with a financial advisor or planner who will guide you through a process of combining life insurance, annuities, stockholdings, mutual funds, bonds, and money market instruments to create a good plan. A good one will also help you to do a WILL that chronicles your desires, sometimes while you are still alive (Living Wills), or after you are dead.

As with any goals in life, wealth building and transferring to your heirs require intentional decision making through actions and behaviors that drive you to achieving those goals. Your company ultimately becomes the vehicle that drives your dreams for wealth creation and passing meaningful legacies to your children and theirs. As Proverbs 13:22 teaches us, "A good person leaves an inheritance for their children's children, but a sinner's wealth is stored up for the righteous." (Bible verse of the New International Version, NIV). I grow goose bumps whenever I feel like I am not close to fulfilling this Godly requirement. I believe that for many Christian entrepreneurs, this demand is one of the cornerstones of their life and what they go out to do day in, day out.

[1] Man Crashes Plane Into Texas I.R.S. Office - The New York Times (nytimes.com)

[2] Real Time Billionaires (forbes.com)

CHAPTER 13

Scaling your business and diversification

Whatever the mind of man can conceive and believe, it can achieve.

Napoleon Hill, American self-help Author

    The true test of a growing business is its ability to multiply, grow and reproduce its success. And once that growth becomes evident, any entrepreneur worth his salt will not rest on his oars. This would be the time to go back to the drawing board to find out more ways to make your product better and more suited for the finer tastes of your customers. Because the truth is, we live in a world where trends are a constant; attention spans are noticeably short, and people are fickle. So, your products will not always be the hottest thing in the market for exceedingly long. When you get to the top, it is then that you should work harder to remain there and more relevant to your customers. This is a process that requires reengineering and rediscovery. In today's business climate, transformational entrepreneurs are always on the cutting edge of advancing change and seizing the opportunities in the competitive landscape to gain leadership for their companies.

    Getting to this point in your business gives you an exhilarating feeling, knowing your business has risen to so much relevance and success that the results are evident. But resting on your laurels would be a disservice to that business and every one of your employees who have invested their time, resources, and knowledge into making your business better. The next important step, therefore, is to upscale and diversify.

To many business owners, "scaling" and "diversification" probably sound like too much grammar but they are necessary to keep your business alive for the long haul otherwise you may become stagnated and rot. Upscaling is the process of increasing your market value so you can appeal to the finer senses of your clients or get access to a more exclusive market. You can do this by rebranding your business, moving to a better office location, or hiring more qualified staff. These things are challenging, and we will talk about them in more detail as the chapter progresses, but they would ensure that the value of your business skyrockets and you remain on the map longer.

Diversification on the other hand is a growth strategy that involves entering new markets and industry, especially one that your business does not currently operate in. You can do this by producing new products that are not in the category that you were known for before, or you can buy shares in the said other business market or just invest in these other businesses. Most entrepreneurs do this when they not only want to stay ahead but want to stay afloat in the event of economic emergencies or meltdown that could sink their business. The basic idea is to expand your reach into other markets that do not negatively react to the same economic downturns as your current business would.

There are several diversification strategies that one's business could go through, including the following:

Horizontal Diversification: This is the development or acquisition of products or services that complement your original business ideas or your products or which generally appeal to your current customer base. Let us take for example that you have built a construction business, then you decide to start making your own cement; this would need a lot of equipment and facilities to diversify into that business, but then it would appeal to your existing customers and complement your original business.

Concentric Diversification: This involves adding new products that have technological or marketing synergies with your existing product lines or industries but appeal to new customers and can draw them into your circle. A perfect example was when Apple inc. who sold laptops and smartphones decided to start producing the new air pods.

Conglomerate Diversification: This sort of diversification is rife with risk of failure, but if it succeeds, it not only brings you a new customer pool, but it also helps you stay afloat longer. This type of diversification occurs when you add on new products and services that are in no way related to the products and services that you were previously offering. This would take a lot of time, resources and money, money to buy new equipment and technology that could be used to make these products. A perfect example would be the Dangote Cement of Nigeria which has diversified into the food business.

Vertical Diversification: This kind of diversification can also be called integration. Vertical diversification entails expanding your business in a backward or forward direction along the production chain of your product. It does not require new technology as you already have all you need right there. With this approach or type of expansions, you may decide to control more than one stage of the supply chain. This involves little risk for the business as it is basically the same product you are selling, only with more control of the market outcome.

Like I said somewhere in the beginning, deciding to diversify your business will require a lot from you. It is not a step-in business that can be taken lightly, or it could put your business in a difficult situation, trying to pay for a wrong decision with the profits of the core business products. There should be extensive market research conducted for the new product or service, there should be a thorough assessment of your client's needs and preferences as it will hurt your business if you neglect already loyal customers in the pursuit of new ones. You could do these assessments by online paid/ sponsored surveys or by social media feedback. You could also develop a clear and concise product development strategy and then test the market on the sample products. Many companies do this by paying some random people to test out the products and get feedback from them. You can also do this by finding out how well your sales department, marketing and supply chain operations can keep up with the added demands for the new products and services.

If this diversification is done well, you will have added so much value to your company that your shares will increase in value overnight. It could also generate new streams of revenue for your company and limit the impact of sudden economic changes in the market for you and your business.

Upscaling on the other hand is a lot more refined and requires a gentler inside hand. Every kind of business growth is risky but sitting down to plan and come up with a sustainable business growth strategy can help minimize those risks and make sure your business is growing in the right direction.

The first step in upscaling your business is to assess your employees. The first thing people might notice about the quality of your business going up would be your products and then your employees. If you are working with people who cannot adapt really well to change, it may mean that your company would not survive the transition. You actually get your money's worth when it comes to your employees and when you get the right people who are qualified and are satisfied with how much compensation they receive; you will have done more upscaling in that one move than some companies are willing to do in a whole decade.

But more than getting staff that can adapt to change, provide them with opportunities for personal development schemes that could help them scale the progress ladder up. This one step will convince your staff, especially the still skeptical ones; that you mean business and you are ready to aim for the stars.

The next important thing you need to know to upscale your business is that you do not need the most up to date technology today. Those technologies would take time to get a grip of by you and your employees and this may take more valuable time that you could utilize more effectively if you put it in upgrading your products and services. You can retain the same technology that has served you well over the years but with a little upgrade. This is because overhauling your entire technological unit may mean shutting down the business for a little while and this could be incredibly stressful and tasking on you and also make you lose some of your customers.

The next important decision you could make while trying to upscale your business is to try and outsource some of your work. This would go a long way in helping you concentrate on the actual upscaling of your business, leaving the less important tasks to professionals. People always have the mentality that outsourcing is a sort of cheating where you play rookie with your work passing it on to someone else to do. But with the advent of maximizing your time as a businessman and people understanding the value of time, they stopped regarding outsourcing as a crime. Why waste time doing something that takes your time and does not make your business more productive when you can give the work to companies that are experts in handling that sort of thing and then pay them for it? Trust me, the money you spend outsourcing that task will only be a fraction of what you will make when you have used that time more productively in upscaling your business.

I'll close by saying this; growth is a painful and tasking process, but no one has ever complained or died from growing better. These steps may take a lot of time, but they would ensure your business' staying power in the event of any surprises. Learn to be proactive about your business and reap the benefits

CHAPTER 14:

The importance of family

Families are the compass that guide us. They are the inspiration to reach great heights. And our comfort when we occasionally falter.

Brad Henry,
Lawyer, Politician, Former Governor of Oklahoma State

Like I said somewhere in the beginning, my daughter is a great storyteller, and dinner times are arguably the most entertaining and educative meal in our household. I remember a story she told us about a kid in her class, a little boy whose dad was building drugs to cure cancer. It turned out the boy's dad was never at home when they were awake, and they were mostly raised by their mom. This story came to light in the school when the boy's mother fell sick and was taken to the hospital. When the boy was summoned to the principal's office, something strange happened.

The kid's dad had been called back from work with the emergency and he wanted to get his kids from school and take them with him. When the boy saw who they asked him to go with though, he ran off down the hall screaming that he did not know who that stranger was. Every attempt by the man to calm him down and reassure him that he was his father, proved abortive. The relative who was familiar to the boy had to be called to come take him home before he agreed to go with them. "Dad, you needed to see him run screaming down the hall", my daughter kept saying. She added that the little boy told them later 'my mum says not to go with strangers!' repeatedly. My daughter said all her classmates were sad and confused.

While I felt for the boy and could sympathize with what he was going through, this has happened to many entrepreneurs in business. It may not be in the same circumstances, but it is evident that a lot of entrepreneurs have lost their families to their work. I can only imagine the hurt and confusion on the man's face when his son went running down the hall calling him a stranger and causing a scene. Therefore the need for balance in your life as a businessman/businesswoman is very important.

The role of family in everyone's life and success cannot be overemphasized; we are social creatures; we will always have the need to connect with people at a deeper sense than just the mundane. Values like love, friendship, companionship should mean more to us than a whole lot of other things. We crave them and the support they give us, and family is the smallest social unit one has; without family, we could as well not even have a purpose or passion. These are emotions or concepts that are driven by the emotions invoked in us by our families. You are a complete entity because of all these aspects of your life.

Balance has always been one of the biggest problems of the entrepreneur; the need to even out every aspect of your life so that everything falls cleanly into place and you are not lacking in every regard. I will not tell you it is easy because that would be a lie. Building a business on its own is also an extremely hard endeavor; it would require lots of hours spent poring over charts and figures, it would require late night meetings and long conversations held in the workplace or restaurants with people who could make your business better. It is a fulltime job. Then how can one do all that is required of them as an entrepreneur to succeed and still have all the time to spend with their family?

Sad as it is, a lot of people have lost their families, especially their spouses in a bid to experience business success. And while that success may be great and exhilarating at first, it could become hollow and empty in a short while. Because what use is all that success if you do not have people to share it with? That is why balance is especially important for any businessman/businesswoman to attain.

Warren Buffet, one of the richest and most generous men in the United States once said; "Don't risk what is important to you, to get what is not important to you." And this advice I find will always be valid for every entrepreneur in the market. This is because every entrepreneur needs a support system and people they too can rely on. You will agree that when it becomes hard in the workplace or there is a crisis going on, the first place you want to turn is your family, your spouse, and your kids. You do that because they are your safe place, and every safe place needs to be protected and kept sacred. Many entrepreneurs may never have gotten off the ground when they hit rock bottom, had it not been for their spouses and children.

There is also a sort of maturity and grounded-ness that having a balanced family life gives you as a person and businessman/ businesswoman. That balance gives you credence in the society and your immediate community.

A lot of people would argue that there is not enough time for them to succeed at work and still come home to be the perfect spouse or parent. My wife and I started our business in home health care that has brought us a lot of success, and I must tell you that it has not been all roses and unicorns; there was a lot we had to learn and be intentional about.

Let us see a few attributes you can inject into your business practice.

Learn How to Prioritize: The skill and wisdom to prioritize effectively and know what is most important to you is a skill you do not learn just anywhere. It is, however, very instrumental to your success as an individual and as a business owner. It is not enough to say in your mind that these things are important to you, it is crucial that you are intentional about them; learn to write those priorities down. They would gain more life every time you write them down. If this is not done, the tasks that are urgent at any point in time become your priority and you would never get to spend the time you wanted to spend with your family.

Learn the Subtle Act of Planning: As with prioritization, learn to be intentional about your planning. Plan every day ahead and try to strictly follow that plan. When making those plans, that is where you are required to reflect your need for balance. Factor in your family, your community, work details and even your faith. Learn to be intentional about these things; learn to even schedule time for rest and play, no matter how strange that may sound. Those are the things that help you reduce your stress levels and leave you fresh for the next day of work, so why feel strange about making a schedule for them? My most memorable times have been holidays that we took from work to rest even if for only a few days. We have traveled to Vancouver, Canada for a week, Kissimmee, Florida with the whole family, and Nigeria with medical mission teams for rural ministry. We recently spent a weeklong "work-vacation" in Seattle Washington away from the snow and cold weather in our Minnesota base. It was one of the greatest and most relaxing times we have ever had. We planned for each of them a long time ahead. So, plan also opening a new office and hiring new staff, plan for the times you and your staff can come together to learn and train, including role plays and relaxation. As much as possible, help your people to spend quality time with their families. Some companies now have facilities for children's play and have instituted family days at work.

Be Intentional and Committed: The importance of organization cannot be overemphasized. Your physical space reflects your mental state and your private life. You must be intentional and disciplined to follow those plans that you set out to the letter. Without commitment and intentionality, it would be extremely easy to abandon your plans and follow the need of the hour if it is pressing enough. Do not let emergencies that popup be the excuse to not follow your plan and free up that time you set out for your family.

Learn to Sacrifice: The bitter truth that a lot of entrepreneurs I know had to learn the hard way is that you cannot do everything. There would not be time to do everything you want to do; there would not always be resources to get everything you want from your life and your business. I know the glamorous lie that was sold to us in business school; "Learn to work for yourself so you can have everything you want in your life and still have time to do everything you ever wanted to do." The truth is that entrepreneurship is even more time consuming than having a job where you have to work for someone else. Sometimes, you may have to sacrifice that trip that you always wanted to take with your friends to Dubai or Egypt for some alone time with your family. These luxuries will eventually find their way into your life, but while they have not, learn to live without them.

Learn to Work Smart: In our fast-paced world, it has become a thing of pride that you are so busy that you do not have time for anything else. The sign, however, of balance in business is being able to crush your business targets and get amazing results all while making sure that your family is not neglected. You can make this happen by learning to work smart instead of hard. It is basically learning to work with your mind instead of with brute force. You do this by setting up systems in place through careful organization and planning so that even while you are sleeping, you are still earning. I once came across a quote by Warren Buffet that said, "If you don't find a way to earn money while sleeping, you will work until you die." With careful planning, having those systems in place will go a long way in giving you the time you need to rest and be with your family.

CHAPTER 15:

Last Words, TRLT!

There is no magic to achievement. It's really about hard work, choices, and persistence..

Michelle Obama, American First Lady, Wife of President Barack Obama

"**The Road Less Traveled**": As I conclude this book, I am reminded of these four words we often use to inspire ourselves about the enormity of our calling as business owners. "The Road Less Traveled; A New Psychology of Love, Traditional Values and Spiritual Growth" is the title of a book by a soldier turned psychiatrist, M. Scott Peck who believes that "problems must be overcome through suffering, discipline and hard work."

In common language, "The Road Less Traveled" signifies uniqueness in what you choose to accomplish and your tenacity and resilience to stay on course regardless of the difficulties and dangers of continuing. You can say that "TRLT" represents the pain an entrepreneur must go through and endure before they can shout 'Eureka!' I have been through that road myself. I recall when Mariam and I started Dominion Resources, Inc in January of 2009; with no savings of our own, nor any bank loans for that matter, we headlong stayed the course. We had expended both of our small workplace 401(k)s to make a down payment for the franchise we invested in and the myriads of needs for our new office. For another 6 months, we continued juggling between our part-time salary jobs and our new business to pay our mortgage, and office expenses, including a part-time staff, rent, phone, and internet. Our first business income came in in June 2009. But the biggest test laid ahead of us. As we were growing in the few years following, we were racking up debts with the IRS – another topic for another business book! But for the intervention of our company accountant, Tim Schuth at SLS Accounting, Glencoe, Minnesota, who helped us negotiate a tough but face-saving payment plan, the IRS would have put us out of business. At one point, Tim told me to stop taking salary because my salary was better used to pay the IRS debts. By 2014, we recorded our first profit in our P & L, and we have not looked back. I am incredibly aware that each person's story will be different. In fact, I often tell Mariam that not many people can do what we did: waiting for five years to make their first business profit.

Let me say it again; not many people who start a business can stand the rigor of staying in business. If you are already used to comfort and an easy life, if you have enjoyed a carefree lifestyle and everything has been at your beck and call, you may find that starting a business may be too much for you. Starting a business does not immediately translate into success. You must give yourself time to experience some tough times before you can begin to see some fruits. The following D's, which have become my mantra in my entrepreneurial journey would help would-be business owners who may be in a similar situation as mine many years ago. I hope they blesse you in your own journey on "The Road Less Traveled."

1. **Dedication:** This word is defined as being wholly committed to something, as to an ideal, political cause, or personal goal. Dedication is the mother of motivation; and motivation is the harbinger of promotion. You must have the attribute of dedication. It is something you cannot hide away from as an entrepreneur. Other people will attest to your being dedicated or otherwise. You must show zeal and attachment to the position you occupy so that others can speak well of and emulate you.

2. **Diligence:** The online Dictionary.com defines being diligent as being "constant in effort to accomplish something; attentive and persistent in doing anything." It

means painstakingly doing or pursuing your goal with persevering attention. One of my favorite Bible verses, Proverbs 12:24 says, "Diligent hands will rule, but laziness ends in forced labor." As an entrepreneur, you must get your hands dirty so that you can look into the mirror after a thorough wash to say to yourself, "I did not do so badly after all."

3. **Devotion:** Zealous or ardent in attachment, loyalty, or affection: You must show devotion to what you do otherwise you are not going to get anywhere. Another side of devotion is your life balance comprising your family, spirituality, relationships, lifestyle, and attitudes. You must do everything to stay current and maintain a healthy spirit, soul, and body.

4. **Discipline:** The way you work, or your work ethics determines the success or failure of your business. You must be highly disciplined in your role so that you can be relied upon to become a leader in your work and maybe even community. Inc. magazine recommends "8 Key Disciplines Every Business Owner Needs for Success" (1). They include mental toughness, letting your business plan guide you in your progression, demonstrating a sense of urgency, and treating every dollar as if it is personal. Nothing can be truer than these. Your business is you, and your name is on the door, although may be unseen by anyone. The way you run the show will make a lot of things happen, positively for the success of the business, or negatively for its failure.

5. **Doggedness:** Do you get easily disappointed by temporary setbacks or losses? Most businesses grow out of difficult and challenging seasons as the owners and managers find teachable lessons in trials. The mercurial founder of Apple, Steve Jobs, was initially thrown out of the company by his Board of Directors but later when the company was shuttering, he found his way back and

went on to invent the great technological phenomena of our generation, the iPod, which then led to the iPhone and iPad. You must embrace trials and challenges before you can breakthrough in your area of interest. But you must be dogged and tenacious.

6. **Drive:** Let me ask you a silly question. How does a car move? Dur, you might say! A car moves by being put to drive, by someone! Even self-driven cars, an emerging technology, must be activated for it to drive. Believe me, you can have a freshly mint, custom made Lamborghini, Mercedes, or Cadillac worth over a $1 million. The shining piece of metal will sit in your garage and nobody will be able to admire you unless you put the darn thing to the drive and go around your street and the highway. So is your beautiful corner office. You must go to work. When a car is not in drive, we call it "parked". You do not want to be parked in your business. Drive, push, motivate and sell yourself to the job.
If nothing else drives you, if there is anything that brings out the passion in you, let it be your business. And just like a car that needs to be driven every day to make it functional, your passion for your business must continue year in, year out. If you lose interest, or become complacent, you run the risk of grounding the business and everything you have built over the years may be lost.

7. **Dynamic:** This word is defined as pertaining to or characterized by energy or effective action; vigorously active or forceful; energetic. Every day must be an opportunity to get ahead in your game, career, or business. You must see opportunity for success and run for it. Keep in mind that for every weakness, there is a potential strength that you can build. Always seek to stand out and muster opportunities and threats in your area of calling for maximum results.

8. **Daring:** Bold or courageous; fearless or intrepid; adventurous. In the Bible, God said to Joshua that if he ever wanted to step into the shoes of Moses (which by the way, were seriously oversized for anyone besides Moses); one thing he would need to lead the people of Israel on the journey to the Promised Land was "Courage". Joshua 1:9: In fact, God told Joshua to be "strong and courageous" three times to make the point clear to the young leader. To earn a position of significance in business, you need to put on the "Fear Not" cap. You must be fearless and bold like small David before the giant Goliath. You may need to break into new markets, geographical territories, a county/government department, or specific company. This may be a goal of a lifetime; so, go for it as if there are a thousand of you preparing for the attack. You must be adventurous before you can be prosperous.

9. **Develop:** As a business owner, you must constantly re-emerge, re-invent and relaunch yourself through education, awareness, and intentional personal growth. This is not just about enrolling in a business school, which is beneficial if you can afford it money and time wise, but literally seeking to know your business more and more every day. We live in a generation of unrelenting, constant changes. Most businesses that I know are highly regulated and the laws and legislations have always been rewritten at the state and federal levels of congress. On top of the issue of compliance with the laws is the never-ending breakout in technology. For the avid leader, these things can be overwhelming, but you cannot give up or throw in the towel. If you do, you will suffer for it one way or another in the future. In 2017, I interviewed with the Small Business Administration in Minneapolis to get a spot in the yearlong "Emerging Leaders Street MBA" program. The instructions were priceless and the inspiration unimaginable. You cannot attend a business education program and not impact

your organization positively. Attend conferences, seminars and seek membership of your local chamber. They often offer lots of growth and development opportunities in exchange for the membership fees.

Find books to read on your industry and general topics of interest. Since we all have our mobile gadgets, find useful apps in the app stores that could help you to follow trends in your industry and most especially, technology. Follow great leaders and entrepreneurs like Barack Obama, Bill Gates, Warren Buffet, and Oprah Winfrey to know which books they are reading. Subscribe to audio books like Blinkist (which summarizes whole books into 15 minutes listenable audios). I have gained tremendous inspirations from listening to audio books on Blinkist, some of which I have applied and turned to growth in revenue in our company.

I hope and pray that you will find these attributes helpful to propel you to the next level of your career in business. As the word of God says, "You're the light of the world, a city set upon a hill that cannot be hidden", Matthew 5:14. Therefore, let your light shine so that others can see it and be motivated. Do not extinguish the candle, let it be a source of illumination to everyone around you. May your experience on The Road Less Traveled be one of energy, strength, and motivation and may you arrive at a destination where you can say, "Thank You, Lord, for bringing me this far."

ABOUT THE AUTHOR

CORNELIUS DIPO AJAYI, MBA,
PERSONAL ENTREPRENEURIAL STORY

A first-generation immigrant, the author arrived in the USA with his wife Mariam, and their three 3 children with $1,000 cash in hand in September 2000. Through hard work, a little bit of "suffering" in the early years, and mostly God's grace, he is growing his space in the American Dream.

At the onset of the 2008-2010 Great Recession, he and his wife purchased a franchise in Home Health Care using monies they had saved in their workplaces' 401k (retirement) accounts. In January 2009, they started Dominion Resources, Inc, a.k.a. Dominion Cares, in Glencoe, Minnesota (www.dominioncares.com). Although they faced uphill tasks of growing clientele and finding money to fund the business, they persevered and after a few years, began to breathe some air of success. In the last 5 years, the company has consistently earned decent profits year over year.

Based on the success of Dominion Cares, in 2018, Dipo and his wife launched an educational nonprofit, Gloria Charities International (www.gloriacharities.org), which enables them to give back to their communities both in the USA and Nigeria through various education oriented assistances and scholarships to students in high schools and colleges.

During the COVID-19 global pandemic, most workers were forced to work from home. As a result, e-commerce emerged as a formidable alternative to in-store shopping. This gave Dipo Ajayi the inspiration to start PLANET AVENUE, an online store providing shoppers the opportunity of selecting high quality own label products curated from around the world for sale on major platforms like Amazon, eBay, Shopify, and Etsy. His website can be found at *https://www.theplanetavenue.com.* Dipo holds MBA Marketing, is a prolific writer, public speaker and sits on the board of several nonprofit and for-profit organizations.

www.ingramcontent.com/pod-product-compliance
Lightning Source LLC
Chambersburg PA
CBHW052327220526
45472CB00001B/303